THE ARTIST AS THERAPIST

THE ARTIST AS THERAPIST

Arthur Robbins, Ed.D., A.T.R.

*Professor of Art Therapy, Pratt Institute
Director of the Institute of Expressive Analysis; Faculty,
National Psychological Association for Psychoanalysis.*

 *HUMAN SCIENCES PRESS, INC.*

Printed in the United States of America
987654321

Library of Congress Cataloging-in-Publication Data

Robbins, Arthur
  The artist as therapist.

  Bibliography: p. 221
  Includes index.
  1. Art therapy. I. Title. [DNLM: 1. Art Therapy.
WM 450.5.A8 R532a]
RC489.A7R59 1986   616.89′1656   86-10466
ISBN 0-89885-439-3

CONTENTS

Acknowledgments   9
Preface   11
PART I.   THEORY AND TECHNIQUE   19
   1. **A Theoretical Overview**   21
      Interrelationship between Aesthetics and the
Therapeutic Process   22
      Object Relations Theory and Its Classical
Roots   24
      Creation of a Holding Environment via
Empathy, Transitional Space, and Play   27
      Use of Aesthetics of Therapeutic
Communication in the Case of Bob   28
      Interrelationship between Images and Words
in the Therapeutic Relationship   36
   2. **Technique as a Mirror of Theory**   38
      Ongoing Interplay of Diagnosis,
Developmental Issues, Aesthetic
Reorganization, and Technique   38
      Guiding Principles for Introducing Verbal or
Nonverbal Interventions   46

Therapist as Educator 42

Self-Disclosure and Physical Contact by
Therapist 43

Developmental Diagnosis and Technical
Considerations 44

States That Cross Developmental Lines:
Depression, Obsesssional Compulsiveness,
Passive Agressiveness, Substance Abuse 53

Special Considerations in Working with
Children 56

Adolescence and the Adolescent 58

Terminal Patients and Their Families 59

Conclusion 60

3. **Holding Environment as Frame for Theory
and Technique** 61
*by Arthur Robbins, Betty Costa, Pia Mitchel,
and Michaela Rowan*

Paired Exercise Series 81

4. **Aesthetics of Healing within the Inner
Representational World** 89
by Arthur Robbins and Priscilla Rogers

5. **Materials as an Extension of the Holding
Environment** 104
by Arthur Robbins and Donna Goffia-Girasek

Form 106

Texture 106

Color 107

Volume 110

Space 111

Movement 112

Abstraction 113

6. **The Institution as a Holding Environment
for the Therapist** 116
by Beth Gonzalez Dolginko and Arthur Robbins

Personal Identity as a Creative Arts Therapist 118

The Intern in the Institution 122

The Treatment Team and Supervisors 129

Countertransference 133

Conclusion 134

7. The Use of Visual Perception as an Aide in
    Planning Short-Term Treatment Goals   137

PART II. CLINICAL APPLICATIONS   145

8. Transference and Countertransference
    within the Schizoid Phenomenon   147
    Jan   152
    Rebecca   159
    Bob   165
    Summary   172

9. Regeneration of the Potential Life Space of
    the Antitherapeutic Patient   175
    Case 1   179
    Case 2   182
    Case 3   184

10. A Study in the Aesthetics of Pain, Rage,
     Loss, and Reintegration   187

11. A Final Word   212

Appendix   215
References   221
Index   223

ACKNOWLEDGMENTS

I owe a very special debt to Trudie Loubet, my editor, who ha. played a considerable role in helping to shape this text.

I want also to thank the graduate art therapy students who attended the following courses: Intergroup Relations, Materials, Introduction to Art Therapy, Advanced Seminar. Their art material and comments were essential to the very fabric of this text.

The following journals have generously permitted me to include in this text material that has originally appeared in these publications: *Art Therapy*, "The Struggle for Self-Cohesion: An Analytically Oriented Art Therapy Case Study," Volume 1, Number 1, October 1984. Reprinted with permission of American Art Therapy Association, Inc. Copyright 1984. *The Arts In Psychotherapy*, "A Creative Arts Approach to Art Therapy." Volume 11, Number 1, Spring 1984. Also in *The Arts in Psychotherapy*, "Integrating the Personal and Theoretical Splits in the Struggle Towards an Identity as Art Therapist," 1982, Volume 9, pp. 1–9. *American Journal of Art Therapy*, "Transference and Countertransference in Art Therapy," 21:1. Reprinted by permission of Eleanor Ulman and Vermont College of Norwich University.

I would also like to express my appreciation to Brunner/

Mazel, publishers of *Approaches to Art Therapy* to Rubin, J. Ed., in press; for permission to include a portion of the chapter, "An Object Relations Approach to Art Therapy." All the above references are the author's personal work and have contributed to the overall scope of this text.

I am also deeply grateful to the patients who consented to include their clinical and artistic material. All names are fictitious to insure confidentiality of the material.

Last, but not least, I want to thank my wife, Sandy, for her confidence and support in this endeavor.

PREFACE

It was October of 1963, and my father had just died of lymphoma. It was an awful, emotional, wrenching experience. During the 2-year period of his illness, I had watched him slowly slip away, until at the end he barely had been present. I wondered vaguely if the same type of death lay ahead for me. His father had died of cancer, and soon I was to learn that my uncle, who was also my analytic supervisor and teacher, would die of cancer. I tried to brush such thoughts aside as I immersed myself in the process of my father's illness and attempted to be available to my family in whatever way possible.

When my father died, I was numb, although I would occasionally break into tears (Robbins, 1982)[1]. At the time, I attended classes at a sculpting studio and wondered if I could identify and sort out my feelings regarding his death through work with clay. The studio was a place where I received per-

---

[1]Some of these issues were discussed in a different context in Author Robbins "Integrating the personal and theoretical splits in the struggle towards an identity as art therapist." *The Arts in Psychotherapy*, vol. 9, 1982, pp. 1–9.

mission to be completely myself; to immerse myself in the smell, dirt, feel of my medium. Here, totally involved in the art form, I often felt a sense of meditation and healing. As my hands grappled with the clay to try to capture the essence of this intense period of my life, I got my first glimpse of how art could be used in therapy. I slowly watched my sense of death emerge, as did a head with deep, hollowed eyes and a mouth reaching endlessly inward. Hollowness, emptiness, loneliness, as well as my ultimate despair worked their ways into the clay. As I dug my nails deeper into each crevice, I felt a release, a strong connectedness with my piece (Figure P-1).

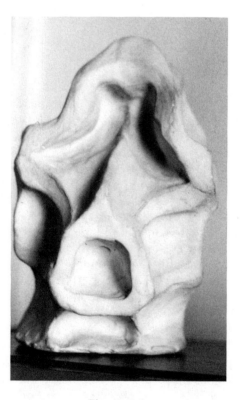

Figure P-1.

I decided to take the piece to my analyst to help me understand it better. I remember how he picked up the piece and felt various parts in his hands. Then, to my surprise, he commented, "You know, everything is so balanced, so controlled. One side is exactly like the opposite." He went on to wonder if the piece reflected an internal sense of being too balanced, controlled, and fair.

I blurted out that I had been struggling with my feelings, or lack of them, and felt guilty at not being depressed. He questioned whether there was something else behind the balancing control. Under the probing I admitted that I felt a sense of relief at being released from the burden of caretaking and the emotional drain of my father's illness. I also recognized that I wanted to get on with my life. What especially struck me about my analyst's approach to my piece was his awareness of and sensitivity to my defenses as well as my mood and affect, and it was that very sensitivity to my defenses that helped me to see beyond the manifest in my image.

From that very personal perspective I came to see how working with art materials could promote the healing that comes from playing with one's personal symbols and also protect one's defense system from excessive pressure.

In retrospect I view that sculpture as an attempt both to detach from and to connect with the image of my father. I, like my analyst, am now disturbed by the contrived, artificially balanced top of the sculpture. It lacks energy or meaning; it has a lifeless quality. I recognize the aesthetically dead spots as the controlled, conforming side of my father, from whose force I needed to disengage if I were to touch and express my true self. At that time, however, I was too frightened to differentiate truly from the aspects of him that were both inside and out, the parts of each of us that were evolving and changing.

On the other hand, there are aspects of the sculpture that still feel alive. For one thing, I am comfortable with the soft lines I know so well and can feel in my own face and hands. They are his and live on in me. The texture and contours of those lines are an extension of the many "me's" who have evolved with time. Also, the symbols of the circle and empty spaces have continued to be part of my artistic work. They express an insulated, blanked-out self surrounded by black moods of depression; the schizoid me who will not allow blackness to invade the self and as a consequence settles for isolation.

Taken as a whole, I suspect that if I were to do a piece today exploring life, death, and separation, I would express myself differently.

As with all sons, the death of my father marked a turning point in my life decisions. Fortunately for me, there was a reservoir of love and care between us that made it possible for me to move on with a minimum of guilt and self-destructiveness. After my father's death I became a part-time teacher of psychology for art students at Pratt Institute. Before I knew it, I became immersed in the development of the new profession of art therapy as I found myself writing, teaching, and exploring connections between art and therapy.

Thinking back, I can easily speculate as to other motivations, aside from my experience with the death bust, regarding my shift in professional investment. Both my mother and my sister belonged to the world of art. Together they formed a closed unit involved in decorating and design. When I was younger, I felt excluded from that relationship and accepted my role as the dirty, messy boy who remained in the sandbox alone, building castles and exploring secret fantasies through sand play. I never felt I could join the world of art, for I could hardly draw a straight line or make "pretty" pictures.

With the help of analysis, I went back to that lost battleground and discovered that beauty could arise out of disorder and that mess was often the prelude to beholding new solutions for old problems. As I reached adulthood, art was no longer the exclusive world of mother and daughter. In the process of working through this very consciously accessible area, I uncovered something rather unexpected. I had managed to overlook completely the central role my father had played in my family's involvement in the world of aesthetics. He was part of an industry that hardly exists today. He manufactured artificial flowers for dresses and hats, and he played a major role in designing and marketing them. Although the style of dress has changed and there is little room for those articles in current fashion, at the time they were the vogue and provided an adequate living for us. They also served as the focal point for discussions with my mother and sister as new creations were unveiled. Again, I often felt excluded from that world. What could a messy, dirty kid offer in the midst of such elegance?

I smile to myself, for even as I assumed a chairpersonship of a major graduate art therapy department within an art school, the small boy in the sandbox lived on. I saw myself as marketing a new profession—art therapy—that never quite "fit in" philosophically in the art world.

From my personal analysis I moved on to become a psychoanalyst myself, ever evolving as a sculptor as well. In the past I have described a good analytic session as being similar to a work of art. In the deepest sense of the word, psychoanalysis can be a profoundly healing experience in that the process brings together and encourages reorganization of parts of the self. Here creativity and healing cross. Many artists find that their art becomes a way of maintaining themselves, of healing their inner souls as well as those of humanity. For myself, sculpting is a place where my mind and body are one and at peace. Furthermore, I become one with the world around me, wounds of the day drop away, and intellectual controls become part of a total flow of process rather than something disjointed from body awareness.

Now in my mid-fifties, at the Eriksonian life-crisis level of synthesis, I find a major drive within myself to put things together. In retrospect, I am particularly aware of how my past personal issues with aesthetics have been reflected in my conceptualization of the theory and technique of art therapy. The art in art therapy was never integrated into a truly cohesive theory of practice. With professional roots as a psychologist and psychoanalyst, it was easy for me to see art as a bridge, of sorts, in patient–therapist communication. What that notion of art's role in therapy has done, however, is to create professional identity problems for my students and colleagues because it blurs the differentiations between art therapy and other psychotherapies. It does a real disservice to downplay the importance of aesthetic sensibility as fundamental to the role and function of an art therapist.

This text is an attempt to mend the split by weaving object relations theory and principles of art and creativity into a cohesive conceptualization. The basis for that attempt is the premise that principles of aesthetics and psychodynamics used together are invaluable aids in facilitating the therapeutic process.

One of the implications of this approach of this approach is that the traditional methods of teaching psychology to artists must be redefined if those artists are to preserve their identities as art therapists. In the same way that art can be developed only as an organic part of the artist in a studio environment, so too must psychology for art therapists be taught and learned within an artistic framework so that the psychodynamic and aesthetic counterparts can be truly integrated. It is desirable for the student to explore, through artistic expression, personal experiences associated with significant self–object internalizations, facets of therapeutic process, and aesthetic equivalents of psychological issues. As a result, I have incorporated into this text a number of exercises that demonstrate how psychological theory and aesthetic expression come together in the learning and practice of art therapy.

I do recognize that there are some obvious risks to such a method of learning. Students can come to feel overwhelmed, their privacy invaded, unless a class atmosphere of care and trust is established, with respect for the defenses and vulnerability of the students. I am convinced, after many years of being a trainer of art therapists, psychologists, and psychoanalysts, that what is gained from this method of teaching is well worth the possible risks. In spite of what we wish were true, personal therapy does not always remove the blocks that interfere with learning. As important as it is to deal with underlying issues, all too often what is gained in the privacy of a therapist's office is not a complete working through of the deep and pervasive emotional currents that can get in the way of learning the very complex subjective/objective material. Exercises, like those included in the chapters that follow, help mend the splits between issues and application as well as forestall the detached intellectualism that can impede the therapeutic process.

In having shared some of my personal struggle in developing a cohesive theory of practice I hope I have demonstrated to some degree how one's subjective inner life can effect the development of a theory and practice of art therapy. My hope is that you, the potential student, will join me in taking the risk of learning this most challenging profession.

Arthur Robbins, Ed.D., A.T.R.

Part I

THEORY AND TECHNIQUE

Chapter 1

A THEORETICAL OVERVIEW

In therapy, patients and therapists alike are engaged in finding the artists within themselves. The therapeutic process for patients is an ongoing struggle to discover true inner representations and symbols and then give them form in terms of developing richer, more congruent living realities. Therapists tap the artists within in the ongoing process of maintaining the individual holding environments that will provide the space, energy, and impetus for patients to change. Together, patient and therapist create a matrix in which verbal and nonverbal communications come alive as both parties are touched by common experience. This complicated mode of interaction takes on a form similar to a symphony or work of art, where multiple levels of consciousness and meaning exist simultaneously. The therapeutic and creative processes clearly have many parallels here. This text will explore the interrelationships between aesthetics and psychodynamics as they relate to the use of materials, the varying developmental issues in different diagnostic categories, actual clinical cases, the importance of a therapist's working with his/her own inner symbols, and the turning of surviving into thriving in short-term treatment placements and institutions. Throughout, emphasis is placed on the premise that all psychological phenomena have their aesthetic counterparts and that incorporating those elements facilitates the therapeutic process.

Interrelationship between Aesthetics and the Therapeutic Process

When I speak of aesthetics, I am referring to making the inanimate animate, giving form to diffuse energy or ideas, breathing life into sterile communication. *Communication* is a key word here, for a completed work of any medium becomes art only when it touches us as living truth. That happens when it is an authentic expression of the artist, and most often it involves an integration of polarities. The most common of such dialectics is that of fusion and separateness. As our earliest developmental struggle between the wish to merge with mother as well as to be separate, individual identities, that theme repeats itself throughout development and with any number of permutations.

It is interesting that the aesthetic and therapeutic processes themselves reflect the same integration of fusion and separateness. My personal experience as a sculptor has shown me that when I work I am one with my stone and apart. I experience image, energy, and cognition as a totality, my mind and body one. Similarly, I am completely *with* a patient while separate, working simultaneously on primary and secondary process levels, as I experience the energy of primitive unbound images and also give shape and form to my perceptions. Both as therapist and as artist I see my "work" constantly being shaped and reshaped by perceptions that become increasingly differentiated through the play of form and content.

The evolution of secondary process is developmental in nature. From birth we struggle to transform our sensations and affects into symbolic form. That secondary process symbolization becomes the basic glue in developing a self that maintains continuity among past, present, and future. As we develop and grow, we heal our splits, integrate opposites into symbolic form, and work toward individuation. When symbolic form includes multiple levels of communication and transcends its individual parts to communicate a larger meaning, it approaches the level of aesthetic communication. (For expansion of this complicated process, see Deri, 1984).

Some clarification and distinction must be made here between an art expression as a defensive statement of the artist and an aesthetic integration of symbolic form in the ongoing identity process. Certainly we can all cite instances of artists whose work precariously holds them together and whose personal lives are anything but integrated and sane. All too often, in fact, the psychological implications of one's art are unconscious or dissociated from self-expression. In art therapy, on the other hand, we are constantly working to make aesthetic expression a complement to self-expression in one's relationship with others. In that process, the art therapist works with an individual's character defenses and slowly helps him to digest emotionally the full impact of the symbolic communications so that there is a real awareness of what is being said in symbolic form and of how the client can manifest that in his ongoing relationships with others. That implies a considerable working through, which becomes the province of the art therapist.

Because symbolization and aesthetic form are developmental in nature, failure to attain a certain level or continuance of gaps in development show up clearly in an individual's art. Furthermore, the variations and complexities of aesthetic form are the mirror showing the variety of symbolic solutions to the developmental crises that are inextricably involved in the quest for self-differentiation. Pathological solutions such as splits, disparities in opposites, and the like will have aesthetic parallels in such areas as overbalances in color or shading, the expansion or contraction of space, rigidity of form, and the flow and organization of energy. Again, it is the artist in the therapist who keys into deadness in color or form and then looks beyond the hollowness or lack of energy to ascertain the psychodynamics being reflected.

Object Relations Theory and Its Classical Roots[1]

With my training as a psycholanalyst, I organize my perceptions of psychodynamics in terms of object relations theory, and therefore that theory provides the framework and vocabulary for this text. I would like to make it clear, however, that when I talk about object relations theory, I am not referring to a unified theory that can be found in a single book or that is espoused by a particular theoretician. My use of the term reflects my own distillation from a body of theory, itself derived from classical psychoanalytic theory. I hasten to add that my framework overlaps into such areas as Gestalt therapy and Jungian theory.

The term *object* carries an unfortunate connotation to those not conversant with psychoanalytic theory. Originating in classical psychoanalysis, object relations theory presents an organized structure clarifying the subtle and complex interrelationships of self and other that we all carry within us. Other, or "object," refers to the who and what in which we invest our libidinal energy. By libidinal energy I refer to the life force in an individual that is partly sexual and partly aggressive but is more than either. It is the fuel that motivates each of us to reach out and invest in the world around us. Essentially, it is the glue that binds all of us to each other.

Traditionally, psychoanalytic structure revolves around a theory of energy that is tripartite in nature and consists of id, ego, and superego. When I refer to id forces, I am essentially referring to the animal part of the individual that is often reflected in primitive fantasies and wishes. Rarely do we see direct expressions of id forces but rather derivatives that are manifested in dreams and fantasies, the stuff of primary process thinking. Superego, on the other hand, represents the accumulated impact on the individual of the mores of his culture and society. Those forces modify the raw id forces. The ego is the rational, logical

1) Some of these issues have been touched upon in a different context in Arthur Robbins, "An Object Relations Approach to Art Therapy," published in Judy Rubin, *Approaches to Art Therapy*, Brunner/Mazel. In press.

part of each of us that is often governed by secondary process thinking and has strong investment in integrating the demands of outer and inner reality. Here the use of words and organization play an important part in promoting integration between good and evil, rage and love, dreams and reality. Problems arise out of the inability of an individual effectively to organize defenses and adaptations around those opposing forces. An imbalance among id, ego, and superego forces often becomes organized around the oedipal crisis and thereby becomes a pivotal point in treatment intervention.

As we look at personality structure at this level, particularly when the focus is on neurosis, there is a clear sense of an internal me and you. There is enough of an individual self firmly established to form a working alliance with the therapist and actively work toward analyzing defenses, resistances, and transferences. Here the core of the defenses protects the individual from such intense affects as shame, guilt, and anxiety. On the other hand, the pain of those affects does not precipitate a catastrophic reaction within the personality structure, for the neurotic possesses the internal strength to tolerate those affects. Consequently, much emphasis is placed on making the unconscious conscious, as well as modifying superego and ego defenses to make that process possible. The end goal is one of allowing the patient's life space to expand, so that there is a richer symbolic imaginative life that is in harmony with the ideals and values of the individual's style.

This conceptualization and approach to personality organization certainly can be of help in working with neurotic patients; however, as many practitioners have discovered, the "typical" neurotic patient has become a rare bird in the therapy caseload. As I review the patients in my own practice, they fall into the wide continuum of primitive mental states that include psychotic, borderline, narcissistic, affect mood disorder, psychopath, and schizoid; all such patients suffer from deficits and problems in the early mother–child relationship. Those very early wounds to the budding self produce formidable protective defenses such as withdrawal, denial, fragmentation, projection, introjection, splitting, and overidealization. They are mobilized to protect the personality from further pain and disappointment.

The treatment of such a broad range of patients can no longer be seen in terms of making the unconscious conscious. From the perspective of personality organization, we see disparate systems of mental structures that produce a lack of integration and self-cohesion.

Modifying the classical theory, with its core developmental crisis at the oedipal stage, in accordance with the above observations, Margaret Mahler, an object relations theorist, presents a developmental schema that focuses on the first 3 years of life, with its emphasis on the relationship between mother and child and the foundations of an internal me and you.

Mahler's developmental levels (Mahler, Pine, & Bergman, 1975) begin with the stage of normal autism at birth, characterized by a blissful oneness with mother. At about 3 months of age the process of attachment begins with what Mahler calls symbiosis. Slowly, out of a nondifferentiated mass, the me and you inside the infant become defined. As we trace the crucial stages of symbiosis, in which mother and child struggle with separateness and sameness, individuation and differentiation are born, and the child proceeds through the subphases of hatching, practicing, and rapprochement. The child's growth from symbiosis to separation and individuation culminates in the achievement of an identity and object constancy. At that point, which occurs at about 2½ years of age, the child has a firm sense of self and differentiated other and is able to relate to people as wholes rather than as need satisfiers. Significantly, the child now tolerates ambivalence, having mended the splits of good and bad, and can maintain a narcissistic equilibrium by a form of self-feeding and self-affirmation that is unique to him.

For the therapist working with a patient who has failed to navigate successfully these very early developmental crises, the task of treatment becomes one of building rather than uncovering. The thrust is to help patients move from a partial object-relatedness, where interactions with the world are characteristically seen in terms of good breast versus bad breast, to full object-relatedness. This involves such tasks as modifying grandiose notions of the self into more human and fallible notions of life and exposing "false self" structures that cover enormous fears of emotional investment and the possibility of loss.

CREATION OF A HOLDING ENVIRONMENT VIA EMPATHY, TRANSITIONAL SPACE AND PLAY

With this framework, the real relationship between patient and therapist becomes every bit as important as the transference, as the therapist opens himself up and taps the various parts of himself that may mirror, complement, or confront the various internal representations of the patient. In essence, the therapist creates a holding environment in which empathy is the basis of communication. Empathic contact becomes a bipolar bridge that respects defenses while addressing the wish to be understood. Like the creator of a fine piece of art, the therapist who is receptive to the many levels of verbal and nonverbal communication from his patient communicates back on many levels. Taken into account in this process are the different levels of psychic structure, with their accompanying defensive postures, and the personal communication style of any given patient (affective, cognitive, visual, tactile, etc.). Again, as in a work of art, the nature of empathy is metaphorical and symbolic, its messages organized through visual, kinesthetic, auditory, or verbal levels, singly or in combination.

The bipolar bridge created between patient and therapist also can be described as a psychological or transitional space. Winnicott (1971) talks about his concept of transitional space as an intermediate area between mother and child that is neither inside nor outside but lies somewhere in between, bridging subjective and objective realities. Psychological space is a similar kind of area, which is projected both in the therapeutic relationship and into the artwork when used. It is a space where the me and you of patient and therapist's pasts find expression through image and symbol. Those representations express themselves in such dimensions as energy sensation, color, rhythm, volume, weight. Slowly, with the artwork and therapist's holding, organizing, reflecting back the patient's internal pathological state, the patient is given the chance to play with unresolved polarities and representations to find new integrations and solutions.

In essence, the therapist facilitates the patient's reconnecting with what Winnicott (1971) calls primary creativity, or the early illusion of the infant that the world is his and that he can maintain a blissful state of oneness. Ironically, such primary creativity is a prerequisite for individuation and growth.

The ongoing challenge for the therapist, then, is to provide consistently a frame in which the patient will be able to transform stagnant pathological space into creative growth space by rejuggling opposites and finding new ways to combine old and new. Putting that a slightly different way, the therapist is constantly trying to relate aesthetics to developmental issues as he seeks new and different structures to promote individuation and differentiation.

The recovery of early creativity and re-creation of the transitional space so necessary to bridge inner and outer realities is facilitated by play, says Winnicott (1971). The essence of play in therapy involves the capacity to move and work between dual levels of consciousness, often referred to as primary and secondary process levels. Here the therapist loses intellectual controls, becomes non-goal-oriented and open-ended in experiencing and working with the psychological space of patients. In many respects, the essence of play comes very close to a meditative state where one clears the mind and becomes open to other levels of consciousness. Play is by no means aimless activity or simply having fun, although fun may be one of the ingredients. The essence of play involves being open to images and symbols that have their own logic and organization regarding time and place. The therapeutic interaction and art form organize symbolic play and embody the essence of play. Here form and content become one through a synthesis of primary and secondary processes. Involved in such notions are the merging of bound and unbound energies and the subtle balancing of the inner states of fusion and separateness, organization and control. Therapeutic play, then, becomes an aesthetic response that has its own life in terms of energy and form.

USE OF AESTHETICS OF THERAPEUTIC COMMUNICATION IN THE CASE OF BOB

The following case vignette illuminates some of the issues associated with the aesthetics of therapeutic communication, in this particular instance involving the struggle to mend splits in the patient's personality. Notice how both therapist and patient use themselves and their internal artists during the therapeutic process.

Bob, age thirty-five and single, came to treatment feeling lonely, lost, and confused. He felt downcast and despairing in his inability to form a relationship with another male. Angry with the world and beset by a good deal of depression, he spoke in a vague, vaporous fashion, mumbling his words in a way that left me feeling as if I were sitting in a murky fog. I literally felt as though I were at sea without bearings, floating aimlessly, with another person talking at me. At times my office was punctuated with angry sounds as Bob separated the world into the straight and gay, the conforming and nonconforming. I struggled with my tendency to become blurred and lose contact with my patient. Several times I maintained an empathic, related stance by focusing on a sense of my body, thereby centering myself and releasing me from fusion with the patient's regressed state of numbness and depression.

Bob spent a good deal of time in bars, lost in their darkness and hungry for human contact. The relationships he did have were of a transitory nature, meeting men in bars or baths for one-night stands.

Bob wasn't quite sure where to place me, due to a wariness and suspicion of anyone with an analytic background. He questioned whether I could help him since I was straight, whether I really could understand a man whose main sexual orientation was to love other men, and if I would attempt to cure him by taking away his homosexuality. My answers were straightforward. I told him that I wasn't particularly concerned with pathology, nor was I about to put any patient in a diagnostic cubbyhole. I suggested that we could draw and not talk if he felt that would be more helpful. That pleased the patient, and it became the beginning of an art interest that was furthered by art lessons.

Bob needed to get a sense of me, and I had no reservations about being there for him to touch as a real person and by so doing to get a better sense of himself. In fact, that is what happened. With each exposure to me as a solid person with whom he could interact, Bob's vagueness seemed to diminish. The

Figure 1-1.

vagueness and diffusion was utilized as a protective layer to avoid some unknown threatening contact, and the nature of that fear soon became clear when he proceeded to draw and describe his mother and father. (Figure 1-1). The father was described as conforming, rigid, and sterile, with expectations Bob could never meet. It seemed that there was little that his father could offer him. In response, I pulled up the father within me to offer definition, clarity—in short, a firm boundary with which he could relate that would help lead him away from a regressive, fused state, while being less formidable and tight than his father.

His mother presented a very different picture. She was experienced as warm, engulfing, and soft, like some big, vaporous pillow in which he could get lost. Bob couldn't handle much contact with her, but he loved her very much. I felt as though I knew her well from my previously mentioned bouts of struggling with her in her form of regressive inductions.

Bob's adolescence was a painful one in which he didn't fit into any of the groups in his small Ohio town school. Moving to New York, he received graduate training and became a psychologist but never completed his doctorate. He was able to find a testing job, which he hated, and he generally felt burned out. As I first remember him, there was no place for him to go and no anchorage for him as he retreated into the solitude and loneliness of the big-city gay bar scene. For Bob, the bars represented dark, empty wombs.

As treatment progressed, with my constant presence as a firm boundary, the possibility of a new internalization of a male became a central focus in therapy. At the same time, making peace with past relationships and finding new levels of integration became possible.

One day I asked him to draw his father and mother. The father had sharp points and seemed rigid, almost like a scarecrow. I wondered to myself if that scary image was more illusion than real. Perhaps because of the minimal amounts of mirroring and empathy of father for son, the male element within had become grossly undernourished. The mother was characterized by big engulfing arms. Simply seeing those two depictions (Figure 1-1) and the diverse relationships they represented was helpful to the patient.

Concurrently, Bob's relationships with others started to improve. In about the third year of treatment he was able to maintain a prolonged relationship with a young man and started to share an apartment with him. The following is but one slice of a long process involved in the working through of negative and positive aspects of the polarities of male and female within himself.

Bob came in one day and complained about his lover: "He's sloppy and messy and he's all over the place. He doesn't make too much money, either, and I'm sick and tired of supporting him. Why doesn't he get a better job?" I heard shades of his father in the background but said nothing.

I asked him to draw a picture of both himself and his lover, and he proceeded to do so (Figure 1-2). Then I showed him the pictures of his mother and father, and it was very clear to both

Figure 1-2.

of us that he was acting out the role of his hated father. Of equal importance, his lover had many similarities to Bob's mother. The parallels both amazed and upset the patient. He didn't understand how that could be when he had spent so much time running from the image of his father. I wondered aloud whether there was something he was overlooking regarding his feelings about his father, if there were any positive aspects he could find in their relationship.

"No!" he resoundingly replied in my face.

"Ah," I said, "but what about his need to be organized and clear and have some degree of order? Was this all bad?" I asked.

"No," he giggled. "It wasn't."

"Well, perhaps," I said, "there was something you *did* get from your father that was indeed positive. And now," I added, "let's take a look at the image of your mother. What about your softness and looseness? I know you can be soft and tender when you work with children in treatment. And that looseness of yours, where you are willing to take risks and lose control, don't you think there's something positive in that?"

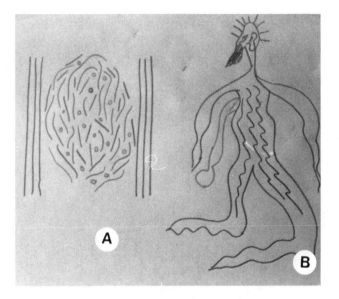

Figure 1-3.

As he studied the parallels between the two sets of drawings, I felt there was now enough definition of self to make it possible to work male and female personae into one image: to help him to play with his internal symbols of masculinity and femininity.

I requested that, and he proceeded with a good deal of involvement and interest, coming up with an abstract drawing consisting of straight and curvy lines and circles (Figure 1-3A).

In the next drawing he tried harder to put the two elements together. The drawing had energy and humor but seemed to bleed out at the bottom, lending a not quite solid feeling to the picture (Figure 1-3B). He tried once again, and his drawing became far more alive and solid, although there still existed a lack of differentiation indicating there was a good deal of emotional work ahead of us (Figure 1-4). This was but an initial step toward integrating the father and mother within him, but he did not regress into his usual hopeless, angry attitude, which was a sig-

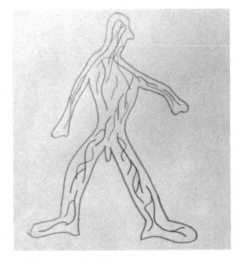

Figure 1-4.

nificant step. Here he was actively grappling with what it would mean to be both structured and unstructured, soft and hard, defined and loose. There was also the beginning awareness that the engulfing, demanding part represented the connection between himself and his mother. His struggle well illustrates the importance of owning the projected parts of oneself; for when they are denied, they come back to haunt the individual in negative ways.

This short vignette highlights the complex nature of the struggle with development and the creative synthesis of life experiences. In this process one sees the constant of life experiences. In this process, one sees that the constant likens the therapeutic treatment relationship to a mother who must partially masticate undigestible food for her child, so that material, like food for the baby, can be assimilated as a working part of the patient's ego. As was true of Bob with his introjected mother and father, patients are all too often overwhelmed by poisonous introjects that cannot be assimilated into the working self. Such introjects are like foreign bodies that loom up and take hold in spite of one's efforts to deny their presence. The art form allows for a safe externalization of such presences so that they can be observed and inspected, perhaps even nibbled at, until gradually they can be reassimilated with new meaning and order.

In Bob's case the verbal dialogue was extremely important in investigating his feelings associated with his father, mother, lover. The verbal dialogue gave specificity to the nonverbal images and an opportunity to elaborate on his perceptions. Confrontation also was necessary, as it was unlikely that this patient would have been able to put the splits together on his own. Confrontation ultimately led to the beginning of a synthesis of perceptions. The intervention was based on the therapist's assessment that the patient functioned on the rapprochement level, had a borderline organization, and was not subject to states of fusion and narcissistic withdrawal. That was confirmed because the confrontations did not, in fact, result in fragmentation of the personality.

In some instances borderline personalities will deny, become angry, or reject the therapist's interventions. At such junctures the therapist must hold onto his cognitive understanding of the developmental issues, maintain therapeutic integrity, and not join the patient in a muddle of negativism and hopelessness.

I'd like to point out here that if I had been inaccurate in my assessment of the patient's developmental stage, the response would have given me an indication of how to adjust the intervention. For instance, if the patient had been in fact, stuck in the beginning stages of symbiosis and his hazy withdrawal was not a regression from a higher level but representative of a shaky hold on reality, I would have observed a far different result. If self and other had been poorly differentiated, a confrontation would have been experienced as intrusive and disorganizing. A good deal of fragmentation would have occurred.

Thus, the therapist's assessment of developmental level and his ability to experience, organize, and reflect back the inner state of the patient provides the environment within which the patient can reclaim a lost experience and find new levels of self-definition and integration. I cannot emphasize too strongly that growth occurs from the process of going through the pain of an unmet stage of development rather than from the therapist's gratifying the patient's hunger. Truly, there is a paradox of treatment: I am with you but separate; I understand your need, but I cannot take away your pain. To rob a patient of his anger, pain, and despair, no matter how well-intentioned, is to do a disservice. When we run from the power of pain, we likewise close off the energy that can transform our despair. What therapists can offer is an empathic holding environment to help make the pain bearable and allow progress and growth to proceed.

INTERRELATIONSHIP BETWEEN IMAGES AND WORDS IN THE THERAPEUTIC RELATIONSHIP

One final point. The case of Bob highlights the complex interrelationship between the world of images and words. Secondary-process thinking, with its foundation in words and rational thinking, gives a structure and organization to the self. Art expression does involve the secondary process functions of logic and judgment in giving form and shape to personal image. However, we need many more structures to give our inner reality a base and foundation that is intrinsically hooked up to outer reality. That transition is a most difficult one, as the image communication can penetrate the defenses at the same time that the patient remains unable to assimilate the inner meaning of the metaphor in his conscious awareness. Changing art expression into poetic metaphor serves as a transition to the world of words and helps to make sense of the truism that although verbal material is strongly connected to reality, not all of reality is encompassed by words. From that perspective different levels of reality can be experienced and understood within the context of nonverbal expression. The art form, then, organizes object relations and mirrors them back to patients. This difficult balancing act of not overwhelming the patient with words that are too difficult for him to assimilate, while leaving room for a subjective experience of the self, requires a constant assessment of the patient's defenses. Often we must allow a considerable amount of time for a subtle integration of the patient's sense of self, before he can put his experience into the complex structure of words and metaphor.

Working with the artist in the therapist and in the patient, within an object relations framework, offers a way to organize the vast array of impressions from the many levels of awareness that make up the therapeutic interaction. The minimal structure I have presented—using the principles of aesthetics to illuminate psychic process—will be expanded on from various vantage points. First, let us take a look at the implications of this theory as it relates to technique.

Chapter 2

TECHNIQUE AS A MIRROR OF THEORY

As much as we might sometimes wish it were otherwise, technique and its applications can never be separated from the larger fabric of therapeutic process to yield a set of canned recipes. Technique is no more or less than the structures that organize the various aspects of the therapeutic process. That process, which describes the unfolding of therapeutic material, is characterized by shifts in levels of perceptual, affective, and cognitive differentiation as expressed in the patient–therapist relationship. Included in such changes are oscillations in defensive positions and movement from one level of self–object differentiation to another. The process can be observed within a single session or over a protracted period of time, as developmental life crises, institutional atmosphere and organization, and choice of treatment modality influence the flow.

ONGOING INTERPLAY OF DIAGNOSIS, DEVELOPMENTAL ISSUES, AESTHETIC REORGANIZATION, AND TECHNIQUE

As indicated above, treatment process is profoundly related to clinical diagnosis and the associated developmental issues that are lived out in the therapeutic relationship. Because diagnosis and developmental issues are so intimately intertwined, it follows that diagnosis will shift right along with the developmental self-object differentiations and defense organizational shifts that occur in therapy. Application of technique, therefore, comes to reflect the ever changing need for new structures to organize a variety of levels of communication as the therapeutic dyad moves through shifting phases.

More specifically, therapeutic process entails the subtle fluctuations of energy that organize each developmental life crisis, so that within every transitional state a symbolic structure arises to shape diffuse energy into a cognitive and perceptual memory of self and object. In more pathological states that continuity of form, or the self, disintegrates or splits away. In such cases energy also gets projected, introjected, or dissociated from the experiential self. Treatment can be directed at the reorganization of that energy into new, better integrated symbolic expressions of the self. Therapeutic and creative processes converge as the therapist constantly tries to organize multiple levels of communication and then create structures for the patient that will facilitate a better integration of symbols or flow of energy between subjective awareness and responses to environmental challenges.

Within that context an aesthetic reorganization of dynamic material regarding the experiences of self becomes an entree for technique, and we attempt to facilitate the reordering of symbolic material into forms capturing awareness of self that contain harmony (the integration of opposites), brilliance (the integration of color, form, and content), and simplicity (economy and completeness).

As therapists we experience the gestalt pattern of verbal and nonverbal symbolic forms that make up a patient's field of communication, and we assess the diagnostic level that organizes such diversity of clinical material. Taken into account are the multiple levels of ego functioning, which include defensive organization, affective states, and the associated representations of self and other. Each level of transference, resistance, and defensive posturing gives us the clues for the level of structure and intervention that can be introduced into the treatment matrix at any given time.

GUIDING PRINCIPLES FOR INTRODUCING VERBAL
OR NONVERBAL INTERVENTIONS

When I speak of intervention, I refer to any input, whether verbal or nonverbal, on the part of the therapist. As a general rule, when we observe the therapeutic process unfolding and progressing, it behooves us to remain relatively inactive. Our job is to hold and to facilitate, and it is only when we meet resistance and the process stalemates itself or inappropriately regresses that we step in to utilize our artistry and expertise to regenerate the self-healing process (for a full treatment of this issue see Robbins, 1980, pp. 43–57).

One of the problems that may well arise at such junctures is a discrepancy between a verbal and a nonverbal modality. Often, more defended and frightening qualities of object relationships will express themselves in the artwork rather than in verbal communications, although one also sees cases where latent strength will appear in the art that has not been observed in the therapeutic relationship. In general, the level of object-relatedness of the verbal relationship should be used as the baseline for making interventions in the artwork. Deep content interpretations that are divorced from the ongoing real relationship can be both threatening and counterproductive. Thus, for example, if a patient were relating to the therapist as a part object, it would be best to keep interventions on a minimal reflective or empathic level. By demonstration and response, rather than by interpretation, the therapist would gradually help the patient through differentiation of self and other, eventually to reach object constancy (where a whole person has been internalized).

I want to note here that although many of our patients require words to provide clear definition and security in the therapy situation, there is another group of patients who experience verbal communications as intrusive and essentially nonsupportive. Again, it is the developmental, object relations level that will dictate our stance. Words are helpful in facilitating the separation–individuation process, for example, whereas verbalization is much less useful for the patient on a fusion level, who requires a non-intrusive, felt relationship before he can use words to separate and differentiate.

Words work along a continuum from concrete to abstract, directional or clarifying, to symbolic or metaphorical. Higher levels of ego functioning are required for more meaningful abstract thinking and verbalization. I underline *meaningful* because although an acutely psychotic person may string together symbolic utterances, they do not serve to communicate, to link inner and outer reality.

True metaphor may be the midpoint for a patient to approach working through material on a more articulate, personal level. It is up to the therapist to ascertain when image and metaphor have ceased to be a bridge and serve resistance, as is frequently seen in inflexible and repetitious use of that style of communication. When image and metaphor become a form of resistance, a structure that creates more verbalization is in order. For instance, if the patient were to draw a picture of ocean and waves and make an allusion to being swelled by the waves of life, the therapist could ask him to depict other people who are swelled or some other experience that would elicit more specific information, more detail.

There are principles that can help guide the therapist in introducing an intervention of any modality or modalities. The following excerpt from Robbins (1984) presents some guidelines or considerations.

> 1. The fluidity or rigidity of the defensive apparatus of a patient to a particular kind of stimulation, i.e., are the boundaries either overly permeable or so rigid as to block all incoming stimulation, and will the inherent properties of a particular medium reinforce or undermine this particular condition. One example is the use of finger paints with a borderline patient. In this case, use of the medium can reinforce a regressive pull towards fusion.
>
> 2. The level of object relatedness associated with any given patient's ego state. Care must be taken, here, in that this can shift quickly.
>
> 3. The inherent properties of a modality such as form, movement, affect stimulation, use of space, and cognitive involvement lend differing structures to the therapist-patient interaction.

4. The patient's unique response to properties such as those listed in 3.

5. The therapist's skill in offering a holding environment using any given medium.

The core issue in choosing any given modality for a patient is determined by the internalizations of early nonverbal, sensory experiences that he or she laid down as memory traces during formative years. Some examples that might shape a patient's responses to various modalities are the rocking of a child in a parent's arms, the singing or cooing of a mother and child to one another, or the playful roughhousing of a father and child. Thus the introduction of a modality may not only affect the ego resources of a patient, like the availability of conflict-free energy or the malleability and adaptiveness of defenses, but also may touch deep internalizations.

The therapist clearly must weigh several complicated factors in formulating a decision. As different pathological introjects are externalized and seek expression, a given medium may stimulate or cool down the therapeutic process. In the face of the tremendous amount of unneutralized affect being released, the ability of the medium to help the patient link up, or integrate various parts of the self must be considered, as well as the degree to which the medium will promote enough security to allow the patient to feel mastery and self-esteem. Robbins (1984) pp. 7–8.

THERAPIST AS EDUCATOR

The introduction of an artistic modality brings up the issue of therapist as technical teacher, although implicit in this question is whether it is ever appropriate to become an educator in therapy. In terms of aesthetics, problems in this area should not be corrected through mechanical or didactic instruction alone. As I have said before, the way any given patient uses color, form, space, and the like makes a psychodynamic statement, so correction often requires the working through of some underlying personal conflict. I would also like to caution that a concern with aesthetics should not be confused with a product orientation. Patients can and do receive a sense of mastery in completing a fine piece of work. Furthermore, some patients flower under instruction and praise, experiencing direct help as a form of nurture and care from the therapist. Others, however, become further enmeshed by their wish to please the therapist and are not aided by direct help. The teacher within the therapist must be used sparingly, depending on whether the patient can internalize help that facilitates self-cohesion and independence or will sink into a passive, dependent, conforming role. In the latter case some amount of anxiety geared at looking for a solution is appropriate and helpful.

That is just as true in instances where the patient seeks a therapist's advice in such realms as sexuality or socialization. As stated previously, there are instances where the patient experiences an educational approach as a form of care and parenting. On the other hand, that approach can easily be perceived as a form of patronization and infantilization. It is a good idea to understand the underlying need for education and information before offering it to a patient. The information itself can go only so far: it can't solve the underlying problems or fears pertaining to, say sexuality or relating to others.

Likewise, the therapist would do well to avoid interfering with a patient's outside life situation. We cannot be gods or omniscient authorities who can project ourselves into the patient's real-life situation and make value judgments of what is good or bad. At best, if we understand what is happening within the therapeutic relationship, we can be of help in giving the patient the courage and resources to alter his outside life situation. I realize that patients do bring provocative material into treatment regarding their outside lives. In such cases we, as therapists, must assess the provocative impact of their actions and respond to the underlying impulse or wish that the behavior represents.

SELF-DISCLOSURE AND PHYSICAL CONTACT BY THERAPIST

Two final kinds of communications I'd like to talk about are those of self-disclosure and physical contact on the part of the therapist. That, like so much else, can be answered only within the context of the therapeutic process. The aim of any communication we give our patients should free or facilitate the therapeutic process. Some questions the therapist might want to ask him before proceeding are as follows: Is the communication for the benefit of the patient or to make the therapist feel better? Will the communication be experienced by the patient as intrusive? Will the communication create regression or a lowering of the level of object-relatedness, which is to be avoided?

In the case of physical contact each instance must be looked at and understood in terms of the impact our physical message may have on the patient, contingent on his or her ego functioning and object relations level. Clearly, contact is to be avoided if the patient experiences it as erotic or threatening. Furthermore, we would do well to look at what is going on in ourselves countertransferentially when we have the urge to touch. At times physical contact can become a means of coping with our own anxiety. That is not to say that physical contact is out of bounds, for we all know of instances when, for instance, a gentle hand on a patient's shoulder is a clear form of support or when a hug is developmentally appropriate. Issues of physical contact should be looked at, however, because they can be multidetermined for both patient and therapist.

DEVELOPMENTAL DIAGNOSIS AND TECHNICAL CONSIDERATIONS

I have repeatedly noted the importance of assessing the developmental level of a patient at any given time before proceeding with any intervention. Diagnosis is an ongoing and constantly shifting process, with the rare patient exhibiting a pure symptomatological profile. For example, the very angry, suspicious, attacking patient may have intermixed in his personality strong schizoid or depressive elements. I say that in advance of presenting a sketch of diagnostic lines and associated technical considerations to make clear my awareness of the disparity between such pure descriptions and the patients who actually walk into our offices.

Horner (1971) gives an excellent outline of some of the

problems associated with each developmental period and connects pathology with issues stemming from faulty early object relations. Problems in the normal autistic phase form the basis of primary infantile autism, which is characterized by a lack of attachment and organization. Proceeding along the very early stages of attachment of the first couple of months, psychopathic personalities are viewed as having had problems in making primitive attachments, although having had a satisfactory initial period of normal autism. Around the fourth and fifth months, when normal symbiosis starts, failures in differentiation create the problems of discrimination of inner and outer reality seen in psychotic states. Schizoid character formation is described as stemming from denial of the attachment started in the differentiating phase of symbiosis. Finally, in the rapprochement stage, occurring somewhere between 12 and 18 months, there are failures in integration and self-cohesion. Problems at that stage result in the borderline and narcissistic personalities. Both types retreat from autonomy, the task of the rapprochement crisis, but they characteristically do so in different ways. The borderline personality tends toward fusion states and a pervasive use of splitting good and bad in his search for the ideal, whereas the narcissistic personality takes refuge in a grandiose self. Although differing in form, there is in both the quest to return to the perfection of an early state of oneness with mother. Also associated with failures in the rapprochement stage are the affect disorders. Individuals in that category have not resolved the dilemma of good and bad existing side by side in one space. All that is good and nurturing remains on the outside, while an immense hunger and greed, which is the bad, stays on the inside.

At one extreme of this continuum of developmental lags are autistic children, who, research seems to indicate, have a constitutional weakness in processing incoming stimuli, thereby rendering the outside world overwhelmingly intrusive and dangerous. As a protection, autistic children create shields to insulate themselves from emotional relations with others. Through hyperactivity, bouncing, whirling, rocking, fixating on their own flipping fingers, and so on, they ward off the contact that is so frightening to them. Clearly, direct and intrusive interventions will not work in creating a therapeutic relationship with such patients, for whom self and other were never clearly defined and the early symbiotic bond never created.

The therapist actually must become the lost object; building, encouraging, structuring a representation of self, but ever so slowly within a well-defined structure with clear boundaries. The "holding" needs to be gentle but firm, with verbalization to clarify and connect the worlds of inner and outer reality.

In a practical sense, because the autistic child has such a major emotional investment in his body, the therapist does best to pick up the child's motor rhythms and ways of moving, mirror them, become a felt presence, and slowly move into the child's world. Working with tactile materials that permit mutual holding, squeezing, pulling, and pushing, can facilitate a symbiotic resonance. However, autistic children mostly show developmental lags in the motor sphere, so care should be taken not to assume that any given child physically can do what the average child of that age would enjoy.

Also having failed to form an attachment in the early symbiotic phase is the psychopathic or sociopathic individual. Unlike other patients with deficits in that phase of development, however, the psychopath does not benefit from a warm, loving, empathic environment. Where others feel anxiety attendant with object loss or disapproval, the psychopath feels nothing. Having taken nothing in, he experiences nothing as lost. There is a sense of cold calculation and contempt about the psychopathic patient, as well as little regard for expression of authenticity, because relationships are seen in terms of exploitation.

The quandary becomes one of creating respect for relatedness and attachment in a person who cannot take in the good things associated with relatedness. The only way to reach that kind of patient is for the therapist to demonstrate that he is more effective than the patient at playing the game of life. In the face of the psychopath's considerable ability to be seductive or charming, the therapist must meet the patient with the psychopathic part of himself that can play with power. Only after the psychopath respects a therapist is there potential for him to find new ways to cope through new identifications with the therapist and finally to find respect for feeling, expression, authenticity.

The very heart of symbiosis has been disturbed in the chronic schizophrenic, and with it his stimulus barriers and perceptions of the world. That renders the outside intrusive, chaotic, disorganized, hostile. Here, self and object are enmeshed to the point of fusion and are accompanied by frightening and suffocating affects. Life has long since been accepted as being composed of despair, hopelessness, and fragmentation. Withdrawal, splitting, and dissociation are commonplace defenses against intrusion, and primary process becomes either rigidly defended against or an overwhelming source of primitive affects and images.

Because such patients cannot tolerate uncertainty or ambiguity without dissociating into confusion and diffusion, a therapist quickly learns that a free-form, unstructured environment is extremely threatening to them. A spontaneous art experience is like being held while falling through space. Furthermore, such patients are frightened of contact, thus affording the challenge to provide structure and nonintrusiveness simultaneously.

Honig and Haynes (1982) are an informative source for therapists dealing with this type of patient, providing an excellent summary of their work with chronic schizophrenics in long-term therapy situations. They structure holding environments for chronic schizophrenics with art exercises appropriate to their levels of ego diffusion. Honig and Haynes employ Gant's framework for grouping diffusion as follows: (a) diffusion of time, (b) diffusion of industry, (c) diffusion of body image, (d) diffusion of perception, (e) diffusion of ego identity. Honig offers one additional category, (f) diffusion of affect. Thus, depending on the level of diffusion that is observed in any patient or group, the authors recommend an art structure that responds to a particular and specific level of diffusion. For patients with body-image diffusion, for example, they recommend that patients draw a mother and child in situations of attachment and separation. Another example might be that of asking patients to depict aspects of their physical rather than social world, like a favorite plant or the house in which they'd like to live. In their excellent article, Honig and Haynes cite a number of art exercises that respond to the ego needs of chronic schizophrenics. In each of those exercises, the therapist offers a holding environment that fosters ego growth and mastery while providing safe structures in which therapeutic material can emerge. Over time the therapist can slowly make inroads into building expressions of the self.

The paranoid patient takes the perception of the outside world as hostile to an extreme. Such patients typically seek to maintain a guarded stance of invulnerability and will rarely allow a therapist to know what is comfortable or secure. Furthermore, expecting attack, the paranoid will characteristically attack first. It is obviously not helpful, therefore, to become embroiled in a combative dialogue. Artwork can offer the paranoid patient a level of control and self-protectiveness while still affording opportunities for self-expression. We must attempt to be supportive even when we feel the paranoid's contempt, arrogance, and patronization. We face one more therapeutic paradox here: we support the underlying need for dependency and closeness in spite of the substantial wall of contempt and disdain. A sense of humor may be our biggest asset in trying to create such a difficult amalgamation of appropriate distance and empathetic support. Essentially, we address the paranoid through indirect metaphors, leaving him many doorways through which to escape as well as return. As treatment progresses, the attacks may be intensified, for relatedness brings forth fears of submission and fusion. The trick is to make the point and move back.

Art forms may not be very revealing, in which case we must assess what affects are missing rather than present in a communication. Therapists should not expect confirmation or validation of interventions, although in the long run paranoid patients may well "discover" our insights as their own.

The schizoid patient has gone through the initial steps of symbiosis and has made beginning steps toward differentiation. Where the chronic schizophrenic has problems with fusion, the schizoid individual denies symbiosis and attachment, appearing empty and alone, with a paucity of symbolization. The sense one gets is of a hungry and needy child who in spite of his needs rejects all overtures of warmth and relatedness. The message that comes across is "I am lost and needy, but I need nothing." Feeling peculiar and alienated, the schizoid patient functions in a state of despair and fear, although neither disorganized nor out of touch with reality.

The therapist's challenge, then, in the face of those conflicting forces, is to create a holding environment that allows for closeness and distance in doses that permit the reorganization of receptivity to nourishment and emotional supplies. Images and symbols, as well as sensations and colors, are offered as a means both to "feed" and to provide a bridge for connection and relatedness. The therapist should not be fooled by the schizoid's initial reserve and reticence, for his sense of aloneness also carries a deep plea for contact.

The therapist, in effect, offers part of his organizing ego to assist the patient in assimilating perceptions and affects while still respecting the underlying wariness of human contact and warmth. Ultimately, schizoid patients must face their connections with denied objects and make peace with their rage and disappointment.

Much has been written about the borderline patient, and the author refers the reader to Masterson (1976) and Kernberg (1975) as important sources in that area. The borderline patient is stuck in the rapprochement phase of separation–individuation. Think back to the "terrible twos" where a parent often feels he can do nothing right. The child, aware of his separateness and yet frightened of his aloneness, wants to go in two different directions at the same time. The dilemma for the child is to separate while maintaining connection. Screaming, yelling, and objecting "No," the child's cries for autonomy are enmeshed with the silent need to be held, a need often rejected when the parent tries to come near the child. In a two-year-old that is understandable. In an adult patient the picture can be confusing and infuriating.

Though borderline conditions take on many shades and colorations, the underlying core remains the same: the developmental issue is one of shifting toward and away from autonomy and using fusion states as a safe retreat from confronting life's problems. The borderline patient moves through a variety of ego states, sometimes being very clear and at other moments losing self-definition. Self-cohesion is a prominent problem.

In their attempts to find magical solutions to their problems, and living with vast amounts of greed and hunger, borderline patients attempt to control everything in their environment. When that fails, they are extremely vulnerable to depressive mood states and feelings of low self-esteem, confusion, and doubt. Strong fears of abandonment are matched by fears of being separate and autonomous.

Part of the picture is tied up with the strong introjected forces with which the borderline individual grapples. In introjection, the patient fuses with an overwhelming or chaotic relationship whose representation takes over the ego. The introject takes over the patient's personality like a foreign body or a ghost from the past and pushes the patient to behave in ways that feel alien. The patient denies or dissociates himself from the introject. Although introjects often appear in artwork, the patient rarely understands the images or the associations he has to them. Regardless of the demonic form such introjects take, they are most often depictions of parents who undermined the patient's quest for individuation in the past and continue to do so through their proxies.

→ Maintaining a cognitive understanding of such issues is of immeasurable help to the art therapist. The patients literally consume both art materials and patience. The task of the art therapist is to keep a very strong and clear perception of what the patient is regressing to when he becomes frightened and "disappears" beneath a cloud of hunger for succor and support. Likewise, structure is important in helping patients maintain a sense of purposefulness and direction in treatment, as borderlines characteristically undermine their progress and show remarkable adeptness in splitting a therapeutic team into warring camps. Along with the defenses of projective identification (identifying with what we project outward), withdrawal, overidealization/devaluation, and denying, the maneuvers noted above are basically used to avoid autonomy and separateness.

The therapist must be prepared to challenge the defenses while maintaining constancy and directing efforts toward self-affirmation and wholeness. Throughout, the therapist first makes the patient aware of the foreign bodies, then helps him play with the symbols of the devils, ghosts—whatever—until, with support and encouragement, the patient can move through the rage, loss, and reparation usually associated with the leave-taking process. As those affects are slowly assimilated into the personality, the patient takes charge of the old relationship and finds ways to make the past serve the present in positive ways.

I'd like to offer an exercise that can clarify these dynamics. Draw four pictures depicting: (a) a relationship you remember in which you wanted to be very close but were equally frightened of the relationship; (b) a relationship you remember that was painfully ambivalent but which you couldn't leave in spite of yourself; (c) a relationship you remember that was so disappointing that you wanted to destroy everything in your path; (d) a relationship you remember that represented everything for you to the exclusion of all other relationships. Try to put all four pictures together into a unity without letting one picture touch another. As you will observe, that is an impossibility. In this exercise you can see the lack of self-cohesion in the borderline individual, who shifts from one ego state to another, one relationship to another, without being able to put all of his relationships together into an integrated whole.

Now ask someone to help you put the four pictures together, but treat the pictures as though they are very precious and you are reluctant to give any of them up, even if doing so would help you to create the whole you desire. That is representative of the problems with which the therapist and borderline patient will grapple in therapy.

Like the borderline patient, the narcissistic character has been arrested at the rapprochement phase and will idealize in the therapeutic relationship, but the underpinnings are different. Where the borderline was not permitted the normal to and fro of closeness and distance in individuating, the narcissistic personality was not adequately mirrored, affirmed, or given a consistent set of definitions by a maternal object; so some patients will retreat into grandiosity, and others will search for objects with whom to merge or idealize. Here the idealization is usually an important developmental step in treatment. Lacking an ego ideal to lend some direction and force to their lives, narcissistic patients need slowly to develop a sense of values and attitudes associated with mastery and competence.

The therapeutic interaction can provide a crucial reparative opportunity to such patients through the real relationship, in which positive aspects of the therapist and therapeutic interaction can be internalized by the patient as he receives the long-sought-after mirroring and definition missed in the early family matrix.

Mirroring means more, in psychotherapy as I practice it, than merely the creation of a visual frame in which to externalize and explore internal images. That alone does not accomplish the therapeutic task of repairing an unattended or neglected self. In my work mirroring connotes a mirroring transference. It embodies many of the characteristics associated with an early mother-infant relationship, that special multisensory experience that exists on kinesthetic, auditory, tactile, visual levels. The importance of the real relationship, which modifies the traditional therapeutic approach of neutrality, cannot be overstated.

In the context of that real relationship a mirror transference evolves that has as its cornerstone empathy from therapist to patient. Within that frame of reference there are far fewer direct interpretations and a greater degree of reflection of the process. Essentially, the therapeutic work is directed toward the encouragement and development of the patient's sense of self that has not been adequately nurtured during critical periods of development. Consequently, the curative power of treatment comes via transmuting internalizations rather than from insight or the release of unconscious material alone.

Following are a number of principles that summarize the mirroring process (Robbins, 1984):

1. The patient's artwork is a part of the total therapeutic matrix, both stimulating and reflecting the patient/therapist interaction.

2. Within that matrix, two minds touch and play as they create a transitional space. When I speak of this "space," I am describing the mutual process of nonverbal communication between patient and therapist, in which they are wholly connected while paradoxically maintaining their own separateness.

3. The artistic mirroring used in building that mirroring transitional space reflects the multisensory mirroring of early childhood development. In the artwork it is seen in such dimensions as space, rhythm, rate, and energy.

4. Similarly, associated mental structure phenomena, such as ego ideal, idealized image, internalizations, and libidinal manifestations, all have parallels in the artwork. Necessarily, they are very personal in expression.

5. The mirror transference does not preclude the development of such traditional issues as competition, rivalry, jealousy, and the like within the therapeutic matrix.

6. The job of the therapist is to facilitate the patient's quest to integrate the various components of the self through exploration, questioning, enthusiasm, interest, and response. Mirroring, then, becomes a joint process in which the affects, perceptions, attitudes of the therapist are of major importance in giving validation to the development of the patient's self.

The interplay of art and the therapeutic relationship will vary. At times the patient may take in the mirroring in the art that parallels the therapeutic relationship. At other times the patient's ability to deal with the much wanted and feared mirroring is so tenuous that it will be tolerated only on a nonverbal level.

Depressive mood states also reflect deficits in the rapprochement stage. In manifesting splitting, depressive personalities have not been able to integrate the good and bad inside themselves and have held onto strong, hostile introjects while expelling all that is good. Sometimes such patients will be driven by compulsiveness to regain a lost sense of self-esteem, with hectic activity and outside approbation. When that compulsive drive breaks down, despair and depression erupt. Art experiences are directed at helping the patient find strength and self-worth through the discovery of his own artistic expression. It is the nourishment found in the experience and mastery that promotes the discovery of the good me that has been lost and fused with a bad internal object. Although it is important for the therapist to be consistently emotionally available, what the depressive needs is to internalize real nourishment and develop an inside symbolic world rather than search for constant supplies of "good" outside to fill up the bad, empty space inside.

STATES THAT CROSS DEVELOPMENTAL LINES: DEPRESSION, OBSESSIONAL COMPULSIVENESS, PASSIVE AGGRESSIVENESS, SUBSTANCE ABUSE

I want to make a point here regarding a number of states, including depression, obsessional compulsiveness, passive aggressiveness, and substance abuse. All five can and do manifest themselves across diagnostic categories, so care must be taken in pinpointing which developmental level is in evidence in making an intervention.

Depression can emanate from a number of factors, depending on the level of object relations and the associated ego functioning. Where there is a deep sense of loss of or abandonment by a maternal agent, the therapist will often experience an amorphous fuzziness. There will seem to be a lack of definition as the patient draws the therapist into a vague, ill-defined sense of despair. In such cases a holding environment offering definition and clarity can add balance and structure within which the patient can recover the self that has regressed to a partial fusion state. In other instances depression can result from a loss of function and a feeling of powerlessness in which case structure may produce a further sense of regression and ineffectiveness. In such instances, the patient can be better met on a mirroring level. A medium that offers many possibilities can best offer a mirror of empathy.

The normal process of mourning, which accompanies not only the loss of loved objects but also situations and outgrown parts of the self, can mimic depression but has within it the seeds of rebirth. Slowly, through the process of mourning, our memories become externalized through a series of painful recalls. With each externalization, we simultaneously reinternalize the loving connections of that memory to help bridge the past to the present. Those connections become synthesized when worked through to form new integrations of the self.

We've talked about the rigidity of the schizophrenic and the compulsive need for activity of the depressive, among other manifestations of compulsive behavior, but those stand in contrast to the obsessive character (or neurotic, if the defenses are decompensated). The true obsessive–compulsive rigidly reduces his life to a narrow position of shoulds and should nots, with the joy of affective expression relegated dirty and unacceptable. Life is then controlled through the magic of aloof mental activity that effectively maintains a mind/body split.

As therapists we offer opportunities for the prisoner to break out of his cramped cell via structures that promote a mind/body response to problem situations. We may well observe the stubborn fight to maintain control, the denial of overt hostility, or the subtle leaking through of sadism. As we play, we introduce messy experiences and attempt to convert the "warden" from opponent to friend and ally.

The major question associated with the passive–aggressive is whether to let a patient ignore or deny his hostile feelings or to confront that denial. The answer depends on the diagnosis. If the therapist is working with a passive–aggressive "character," the diagnosis implies that the character structure is not overcompensated or a cover for an underlying psychotic state. In such cases the defense is ego-alien and therefore must be confronted, the aggression being dissociated from awareness. The therapist can try mirroring the patient's style or artwork in a way that will demonstrate by example the patient's character.

In instances where the diagnosis is incipient schizophrenia or latent psychosis, the dissociated defenses of hostility should be handled with more care and tentativeness. Confronting the patient's defenses, even by mirroring, may stimulate impulses that the patient's fragile ego structure cannot assimilate. The safest course of action is to develop a good therapeutic relationship and gradually to deal with the underlying issues associated with hostility rather than facing the material head on.

Substance abusers can be quite slippery in their use of negativism, avoidance, withdrawal, or evasion when one is trying to make contact. Needless to say, that makes diagnosis difficult. The substance-abuse population represents a wide range of personality problems that demand different treatment procedures. Some patients fall within the neurotic range, some present character problems, and some are defending themselves against a breakdown into a psychotic state. In each instance a complete diagnostic workup is in order to understand the role of the substance abuse. As in the treatment of all defenses, those of the substance abuser must be addressed according to their developmental level. Whether we approach with empathy and support, mirroring, or confrontation will depend on how primitive the defenses are and how fragile or stable the ego structure.

Regardless of object relations level, we will provide a more appropriate holding environment if we get in touch with that part of ourselves that is addicted to one thing or another and use it in our responses. Some issues that are general enough to be explored in art form include the following: me and the world outside, the family I go back to, the problems I face, the problems I avoid, who I am in relationship to someone I care about, what I want from others.

Although tempting, a minimum of personal disclosure is a guiding principle in working with substance-abuse patients. Personal disclosure made to patients with character problems tends to intensify exploitive behavior and can be utilized in the service of power by members of the group. Instead of feeling closer to the therapist because of the disclosure, such patients will turn the information around in such a way as to say, "With your problems, who needs you as a therapist?" A tough mirroring approach that highlights resistances of withdrawal and denial seems more effective than a softer, more responsive stance with that patient population.

SPECIAL CONSIDERATIONS IN WORKING WITH CHILDREN

In my discussion of diagnostic categories and the treatment techniques associated with them I have basically addressed issues as they pertain to adult populations. Although those diagnostic categories also apply to children, there are other considerations because children are still tied to their families in a real way as well as in an internal, symbolic way. Therapists must be careful in dealing with a child's expression of feelings that may bring him into conflict with parents or family members. The content of therapy sessions may at times spill over into a child's family life. A very clear demarcation can be made for the child as to what is appropriate within the therapy session but is basically destructive to one's relationships on the outside. Sometimes there is confusion between what constitutes the communication of feelings and what constitutes acting out those impulses. For example, a child can be told that yelling and screaming at his art images will feel good, but going home and yelling at Mommy and Daddy will probably induce them to yell back, which will only cause more harm.

To digress for a moment, that can apply equally to the treatment of adults. Adult patients confuse therapeutic relationships with those of marriages and families, expecting the same therapeutic attitudes from partners or mates that they get from the therapist. A clear boundary needs to be spelled out for patients so that they do not undermine the treatment process by turning potential allies into enemies of treatment. Indeed, if we are unable to make that happen, we may suspect that the patient is subtly trying to undermine his treatment.

One final point I would like to make concerns the equating of acting out with using art in therapy, as some traditional therapists claim. It is true that there is an acting out in doing art, but there is a critical differentiation to be made when you are talking about the art done in a therapy session. Under those circumstances the art is done with at least some degree of mastery and control designed to promote a mind–body integration. An activity is acting out only when there is little mastery or control in the situation.

Transference issues with children are also difficult to work through in therapy because the child is living an ongoing and developing transference situation at home. We can offer opportunities for catharsis and better ways of coping with the real-life situation outside of therapy. At times we also provide opportunities for new levels of internalizations. How much we really achieve necessarily depends on the assimilation of change into the family matrix.

Therapeutic verbalization with children also varies somewhat from that with adults. Children rarely answer direct questions because their fragile ego resources cannot organize difficult conflictual material. The use of art techniques offers a structure through which to elicit information pertaining to separation while providing distance and protection. Slanting questions toward "how" rather than "why" regarding the elaboration of art expression is preferable for both children and adults. An example could be a child who has drawn an animal leaving its home. Instead of saying, "Why did it do that?" the therapist is more likely to get additional information if he were to say, "Tell me more," or pose further work on the artwork that would give more details.

ADOLESCENCE AND THE ADOLESCENT

Adolescence, as that middle ground between childhood and adulthood, is a time of turmoil under the most normal of circumstances. When true pathology is added to the brew, the clinical picture can become quite confusing as clients bounce back and forth between overstimulation and boredom. It is part of the nature of being adolescent to have wide emotional swings, so don't expect to be able to do away with that. What you can do as a therapist is to face squarely the themes that cause overstimulation, anxiety, withdrawal in ways that can be tolerated and that promote mastery either verbally or nonverbally. That involves, metaphorically, constantly taking the temperature of the individual or group to see where the material becomes anxiety-provoking and then to limit, modify, or withdraw at that point.

Part and parcel of the turmoil of adolescence is the resurgence of aggressive and sexual energy, which may well take the form of acting out. Aggressive and sexual energy requires neutralization and containment rather than avoidance or redirection. Adolescents need to be given opportunities to talk about their aggressive and sexual feelings instead of acting them out. Because adolescents are also often shy or threatened when asked to verbalize such material, art exercises may help to break the ice and provide a basis for discussion. The attitude of the therapist is crucial in responding to the problem. A noncombative, nondefensive approach that is open and direct seems to be most helpful.

The aggression in adolescent treatment situations can easily escalate to the proportions of managerial problems. First and foremost, therapists cannot function in situations where their physical well-being is threatened, for if the therapist becomes intimidated by the possibility of explosive violent outbursts, his ability to carry on the job at hand is grossly compromised. Under those circumstances the therapist should work in rooms or situations where there is direct help available from allied mental health personnel.

Next, the emergence of explosive anger within the therapeutic process is generally not helpful, although it obviously can be unavoidable. The therapist should emphasize that angry impulses should be expressed through words and images rather than action.

In enforcing such structures, the therapist may well come to be seen as an intrusive authority figure. Those perceptions can provide material for fruitful therapeutic work. As in all therapeutic situations, distortions and problems in relationships are inevitable. Adolescents need opportunities to discuss and explore the kinds of authority they can respect, if any, if they are to get along better in their real-life situations. Combativeness, contempt, and disdain are common affects one encounters in working with adolescents. It helps to remember that they are defensive in nature, covering insecurity and deep fears of dependency.

TERMINAL PATIENTS AND THEIR FAMILIES

At the other end of the natural line of developmental life crises is that of helping someone to come to terms with his own or a loved one's death. Although it is not strictly related to the kinds of issues I've been discussing, I want to address that area, which has characteristically been a taboo subject in our culture.

It's not easy for therapists to assess the nature of the denial of a terminal patient. As is so often true, we must take our clues from the patient. Denial of one's impending death is a stage in the process of dying. Sometimes if we provide our patients with artwork that reflects a life review process of significant historical and personal experiences and allows for a final synthesis of personal internal symbols, it will help prepare the terminal patient to face separation and loss. Remember, in our society it is not a common practice to talk about death or dying. Patients may seek courage and support from the therapist to face themselves and their life crisis. Reticence also may stem from the patient's trying to shield loved ones from pain. The best the therapist can do is to assess the patient's underlying motivation and strength to face this life issue, and then, if the denial is not too fixed, to help the patient gently probe the area.

For us, as therapists, working with patients who are enmeshed in hopelessness creates an enormous countertransference problem. All of us are prone to fuse with a patient's hopelessness rather than maintain an optimistic and constructive attitude. Even in the most hopeless situations, we can find some hope in living in the moment.

If specifically working with cancer patients, the therapist can help patients to mobilize their own healing energy through the use of imagery. Material published by Simonton (1978) can be helpful in creating an active alliance of the patient's mind and body in using imagery to help chemical therapy do its job. Imagery work also can help us to ascertain a patient's attitude toward his illness and his readiness to combat the disease.

A lack of physical choices is often equated with emotional restriction and impotence. Depressed patients can easily become fixated on their reality situations and completely avoid the possibility of a rich inner life. Artwork that is directed toward expression and communication can be of immense help in lifting that kind of depression.

In terms of working with families of terminal patients, one cannot stress too strongly the importance of prevailing attitudes of society toward death. As has been mentioned before, it is generally considered a taboo subject and must be approached with care. Patients can hold onto life as a means to protect family members from loss and pain. Preparation for death is therefore a two-way process, involving the terminal patient and the family members. The nonverbal media of art may permit a breakthrough to this difficult area of communication and can be an important vehicle in helping all involved to express grief, loss, sadness, and rage.

CONCLUSION

In closing, I am all too aware that any number of issues related to technique have been left untouched. The principles, however, remain the same. A therapist's role is to keep the therapeutic process moving, and he therefore introduces elements of technique, or structures, to create holding environments that will facilitate symbolic play and differentiation of self and object. The artistry of therapy lies in drawing out the artist in the therapist and patient to keep the process moving through progressions, regressions, and periods of homeostasis. More now needs to be said about the holding environment.

Chapter 3

HOLDING ENVIRONMENT AS FRAME FOR THEORY AND TECHNIQUE

*Arthur Robbins, Betty Costa,
Pia Mitchel, and Michaela Rowan*

Much has been said regarding the holding environment, that space between patient and therapist in which we complement or mirror our patient's inner representational world. Built on empathy, this space will only serve to facilitate the therapeutic process as well as we can dig into ourselves and utilize our own parallel personal experiences and symbols for responses. The process of learning that most difficult form of communication will be the substance of this chapter.

What emerges is a reaffirmation of the tenet that our aesthetic sensibilities are extremely important guidelines in sorting out that most complex interaction of subjective/objective realities. For better or worse, our internal moods, affects, and perceptions greatly affect our capacity to receive and translate communications from others.

What's more, we learn that our life experiences are all too similar to those of our patients. For instance, we may discover that all of us have a sad, lonely part of ourselves that is similar to the schizoid patient, and indeed, if we search hard enough, we may find islands of our own craziness, borderline components, as well as a whole series of constellations that can bring us closer to our patients' inner worlds. We can learn that psychopathology is a continuum, rather than some absolute defined entity. We also may observe the similarity between our defenses and those of our patients and learn how therapeutic expression interfaces with the creative process. Finally, we may observe how our defenses against a variety of moods and affects will interfere with our ability to respond empathically to our patients.

The following represents the work of three students in an advanced therapy seminar. First Pia and Betty drew impressions of a number of personal experiences leading to their uncovering the "patients" within themselves. Then, in pairs, together and with Michaela, they created holding environments for the "patients" exhibited in their partners' drawings.

The students based their theoretical points upon Horner (1971) and worked under the same instructions. The results are strikingly different because of the individuals' backgrounds, experiences, internal representations, and psychic structures. Those contrasts manifest themselves on several levels, from their differing ways of responding to their "patients" graphically to the forms they chose to report their experiences. The reports have been left unchanged except for minor grammatical or syntactical clarifications. You will see how Pia Mitchel is more comfortable with the softer, fusing parts of herself, whereas Betty Costa relaxes into her more assertive, detached, independent self, and Michaela Rowen falls somewhere in between, with intense, deep moods and intellectual distancing. Reflecting that, Pia writes personally and with fluidity, moving easily between past and present, personal and clinical or theoretical. In contrast is Betty's more detached style, with her inner patient addressed in the third person as "X," and her scrutiny done mostly in the past tense. All three generously share their strengths and weaknesses with us, that we too may learn.

Pia Mitchel

"A time when you felt lonely" (Figure 3-1A). I am four years old. My mother worked and I was left in the care of a woman in our apartment building who often left me alone in my room. I recall feelings of total isolation, formlessness, immobility. I had no sense of time; every moment seemed an eternity. The door

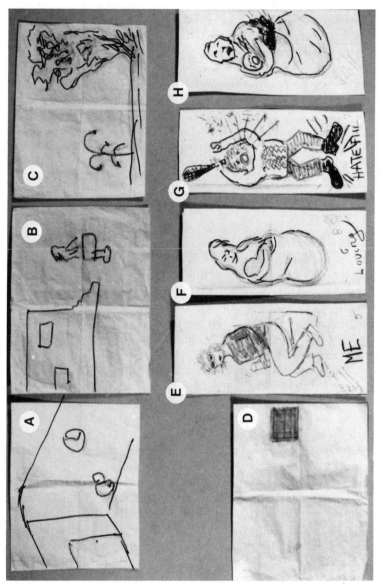

Figure 3-1.

to my self was closed. My only salvation existed in the other, gone away from me. Until she returned, I did not exist.

Once I painted my fingernails and toenails with my mother's red nail polish, and donning her nightgown, I crawled into the comfort of her bed, where she found me, fast asleep. Effectively having identified with the good object, by literally recreating myself in her image, I had defended against the anxiety of isolation.

I recall another time when I fled the apartment building, crossing many busy streets in search of one of my mother's friends, whom I loved. Fortunately for me, my mother was receptive to these gestures and soon found a loving woman to care for me while she worked. "Aunt Mary" held me and played with me and helped me to know that I could survive my mother's absence.

My depressed patients need me initially to be their "Aunt Mary," to provide the comfort they so desperately need in the absence of the good self. In addition, they need opportunities to disguise the hated self–object representation with paint and grownup clothes, in the form of adaptive defenses: to change its image and gradually to internalize the change. My task is to help them find safe ways to explore the dangerous traffic of their internal conflicts.

"A time when you felt rejected" (Figure 3-1B). This drawing, pale and stiff, represents my leaving an unsuccessful job interview. The portfolio in my hand weighs a thousand pounds, symbolizing the internal weight of my self-hatred. I stare straight ahead. I am fighting back tears, terrified that someone will see the worthlessness I am sure of. I am determined never to risk again. If I stay away from people, they can't hurt me. They will never know what a worthless phoney I am. I won't let them.

The schizoid character presents this same stiffness and blankness. I acknowledge them; I do not push. Any attempt on my part to bolster self-esteem is met with denial, suspiciousness, and intensified self-hatred. Unlike the depressed patient who can grieve the loss of love because he has experienced love, the schizoid patient has never been sure of his ability to love or be loved. He operates from a core of inner isolation, the emergence of which is often defended against by a rigidly intellectual, aloof manner. He needs a safe base from which to operate in the real world. Poetry perhaps. One of my schizoid patients wrote

> I am the rock.
> I am submerged in water.
> Sometimes the tide recedes to
> Reveal a shape, which is mine.
> I stand exposed and pale gray.
> All my individual markings
> Dry up and fade away
> In the heat.

With the emergence of this piece, we began to explore ways for the patient to reveal himself without losing his identity. Applying heat, i.e., confrontation, nurturing, encouraging words, was threatening to him. He wrote about his "rockness," and eventually we found ways to chip away, to reveal the beautiful form within the rock. Words, for this patient, allowed the use of his intellectual defenses; for him they were adaptive and ego-building. To ask him to resort to less well-defended modalities would have revealed his nothingness, dried him up, and connected him to his pale gray self, an intolerable realization.

"You have suffered a loss. You need nurturing, but you're ashamed to ask. You hate your 'leechiness' " (Figure 3-1C). I am the drooping flower. Other flowers stand nearby. I need attention, nurturing, and comfort. I'm ashamed to approach them. I hate the image of my depressed self, which stands alone, envying those with brighter colors, fuller foliage, stronger stems. Although I am not dead yet, I droop, disgusted with my spineless self. To mask the depression I rattle on, superficially joining the world of my dreams: I take a class, I join a club, I change jobs, I keep smiling. I look for magic, while inside, the decay progresses and I sink deeper and deeper into my misery.

The depressed patient often presents denial as a major defense. Happy images such as rainbows, flowers, butterflies are covers for the bad, undifferentiated self, which has never been given a voice. To accept those images is to join in the denial. To confront them directly often results in losing the patient. Here the use of alternative expressive forms often crystallizes the affective state. Move like this dying flower. Allow the other flowers to come to you and nurture you. My own experience with the need for nurture occurred last summer in the dance therapy class in which we were asked to "trust the circle," allowing our bodies to fall, releasing control to the arms surrounding us. A terrifying prospect. With encouragement, I let go and allowed myself to be supported, lifted up, and gently rocked by my class-mates as they hummed Brahms's lullabye in unison. I wept like an infant. I weep again at the recollection of that moment. I am aware of just now having made myself a cup of tea. The signif-icance of this image will be discussed later.

The depressed patient needs to be allowed to regress, es-pecially where denial is a defense. Growing out of the state of uncertain autonomy can be accomplished only through a return to the state of symbiotic merger, a shedding of the layers of "false self" being effected through cathartic experience.

"You leave. You run away in the night. You can't bear to be exposed as the inadequate person you are" (Figure 3-1D). The steel box is locked. No one can get in. There are no keys to open it. It is cold, detached, lifeless. It takes up little space. Like the schizoid patient, this form needs to be carefully ap-proached. Too much contact is threatening. At best, there is no response. This drawing represents the nonfigurative interpre-tation of the feelings shown in Figure 3-1B.

"Self-portrait at 11:00 a.m." (Figure 3-1E). I am angry. An-other goddamn drawing! All I want to do is to drink my coffee, smoke a cigarette, and be left alone. Let the student who is pre-senting today get on with it. I wish I had the nerve to protest. I can't. I comply and grumble inside. Later I'll bitch to my class-mates: "What a lot of nerve this guy has, asking me to draw this stuff. I'm not in analysis. After this I may have to be."

My drawing shows rigidity, tension around the neck. I see my frazzled, tired self, half up, and half down, in and out of the experience of being there. I am reminded of the passive-ag-gressive patients as I look at this representation. This kind of patient needs confrontation: to be shown ways to take respon-sibility for themselves. Knowing that the bad self will not anni-hilate the good self if there is an adequate developmental struc-ture underneath, I encourage their expression of rage and I provide clay as a container for that rage. In retrospect I realize that my own unfinished business on the day of that drawing had to do with being confronted with my denial drawing the previous session. Who, me? I'm in touch with my feelings!

"Your loving self" (Figure 3-1F). I'm your nursemaid in this drawing. I'll feed you, rock you, sing to you, protect you from falling. I'll give, give, give. . . . This is the part of me that gets hurt, exploited, used up in relationships. I often end up with leftover chicken soup. Perhaps a projective identification of my own needs is involved here. If I hug, I am hugged. If I hold, I am alive. The patients with whom I've had such relationships and with whom I have not adequately terminated remain as conscious and unconscious concerns. I search for news of them and I'm sad when they are reported to be failing. I want to rescue them. One such patient is a depressed mother of three preschool children. She became a favorite patient of mine. After her discharge I finally found the means to separate when she called me one evening to request that I baby-sit for her! I had somehow set it up so that I had become identified as the nursemaid, quite literally. She was getting on with her life, whereas my role had been extended to include the care of her children.

"Draw your hateful self" (Figure 3-1G). I kick and scream and strike out against the bad world. I'm a two-year-old; enraged, uncontrollable. I want to break things and make a lot of noise. I am unrestrained impulse. This part of myself is frightening and embarrassing to me. Often I feel remorseful after an outburst of anger as my superego demands "adult behavior" in the form of thinking, reason, logic. I don't condone my own expressions of rage, but when my patients act out, I call on the loving mom in me. I comfort them, feed them with assurance. It seldom works.

I remember a time when, as a teenager, I smashed my brother's radio against the wall. He refused to turn down the volume while I studied for an exam. My mother came in, looked frightened at my unexpected behavior, and began cooing and fussing over me. She made a cup of tea. I felt even angrier, wanted to smash the teacup as well! Instead I choked down the tea, thereby introjecting my mother's defense against anxiety. I still make tea, sometimes unconsciously putting the kettle on, as

I did earlier when I was writing about the regressive experience in movement class. I will find ways to nurture my overstimulated, undernourished self.

"Synthesis of loving/hateful self" (Figure 3-1H). This drawing represents the overindulging, loving mom trying in vain to subdue the angry kid. She gets kicked and bruised in the process. The reaction-formation is a defense against my own aggressive impulses. There is no integration here. When I love a hateful patient, I discount his rage, as my mother did. The rage continues, intensified and suppressed in the face of my sweetness (the tea). To call on the anger inside myself more effectively in treatment is a tool I need to develop. If I join angrily with someone else's rage, I can give him the possibility for merger with me as I serve both as a container for the impulse and as a model demonstrating that one can survive that experience.

"Idealized self" (Figure 3-2A). I'd be taller, more luxurious, better developed, uninhibited, open to new experience, and in charge: a veritable Superwoman ready to take on the world. I'd also be seductive and manipulative in a "healthy" way.

This part of me is easily disappointed in myself and in others. Strong superego components exist in this body: intolerance for weakness, imperfection, and lack of responsibility. This part of me does not tolerate the wimpy figure in Figure 3-1E and is critical of the angry kid in Figure 3-1G. She's the source of my projections onto patients whom I see as refusing to get on with their lives. She's the source of my dissatisfaction with low energy and procrastination. The difficulty she creates in a therapeutic relationship is illustrated by my refusal in one case to acknowledge the schizoid core of a patient whom I perceived to be neurotically depressed. All of the tests had come back revealing paranoid features, and the tentative diagnosis of depressed schizophrenia had been made. In my art therapy groups she showed limited insight but continued to produce images that related to her affective state. Verbally, she was unreachable. My expectations and demands of her served only to take her further away from me. I could see the obvious implications of her work. She depersonalized these productions. My idealized self could not surrender this patient to a less differentiated level of object-relatedness.

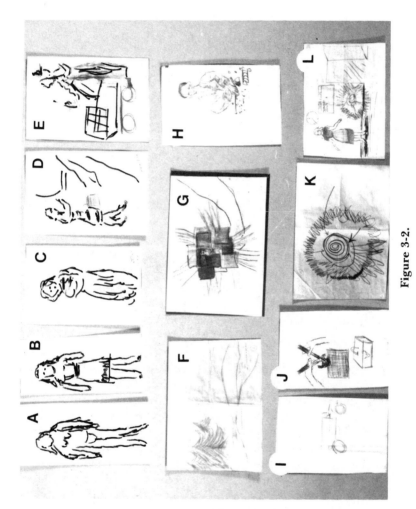

Figure 3-2.

"Ideal self" (Figure 3-2B). Some of the same characteristics are present here, as in the previous drawing. I am more "proper" looking, clothed in socially acceptable attire. I notice that my hair is less perfect, my hands seem to disintegrate, and my fist looks clenched. I seem to be saying, "I've got to do it right!" The dress defensively covers the areas of libidinal power, just as I need to cover aggression and sexuality. Something inside me says, "Don't be so obvious." From this proper position I miss out on a lot of fun. It's hard to play in dress-up clothes. This part of me inhibits spontaneity and is often responsible for my inability to try risky or unconventional approaches with patients. She is "professional" and reminds me of a schoolmarm. She could use blue jeans and sneakers. When working with adolescents, I tend to have diffi-culty going with their resistances and thus meet with further re-sistance.

"The mother inside" (Figure 3-2C). This could be labeled "Introject of mother who makes tea." She coos and cuddles and reminds me of Karen Horney's *Neurotic Need for Love.* Madonna-like, she's a vision of loveliness and guilelessness. She has no feet. She simply floats angelically through conflicts! She has many of the same qualities of the idealized self, but she is not grounded. She is spiritual and is deeply moved by strong feelings expressed in treatment situations. She relates well to grieving patients.

"Working mom" (Figure 3-2D). She too is an offshoot of the idealized self. In this pose she doesn't know if she's coming or going. She looks like she's waving good-bye to the needy ones, while at the same time she seems to be approaching them. She is carrying her tool box (from Figure 3-2I). As a therapist, she works in a "home," which serves as a sublimated extension of her own home. In this role I am not too far afield from the loving mom who stays home and nurtures, thereby successfully sublimating the guilt I feel at having put my own child in a day-care center. As I look at the picture, it really looks like I'm saying good-bye to the children on my way to work. My own mother, who worked and left me, is thereby exonerated.

"Therapist for the schizoid patient" (Figure 3-2E). The pa-tient is the cold steel box on a platform I provide as a movable holding environment until he can go on his own. The two-sided figure suggests an interchangeability of approach. As a loving mom, I hold out a candle to light the way; the other side is a witholding, unresponsive witch. I realize that she is a masquerade figure: dressed for the part, but pretty much useless when called on to perform. What's needed here is some of the angry, kicking kid to shake up the box when a positive transference has been established. The loving mom provides a reliable holding environment, but alone she is ineffective with the schizoid patient. She needs the assistance of the skillful, more objective father within and the challenging, provocative, angry kid. Synthesizing these aspects of myself is an ongoing process.

"Leaving home" (Figure 3-2F). The landscape is cold, with a few evergreens huddled together on one side. The snow piles in drifts, presenting an obstacle too threatening to be passed through. It is desolate, lonely, and bleak. I remember the walk to school on winter days during my childhood. I'd leave the warm kitchen and my warm mother to go out and plow through the snow. The journey seemed endless. I sometimes felt that I would never be warm again. I also associate this picture with my father's funeral in my sixteenth winter. At the time I thought that he would be cold in the frozen grave, and I felt angry at the men who placed his body there. To help a patient deal with loss I reach for these images. I relate through my own experiences of loneliness, bleakness, and death. I offer empathy. A patient I worked with lost her brother while she was in treatment. Through the use of the group experience and her identification with others who had lost someone, she came eventually to accept the fact that he was gone. Understanding is preceded by affective association. As she shivered in my arms, I remembered my own shivering, and I kept her warm. No words were necessary at that moment.

"Leaving a full case load" (Figure 3-2G). Here there is heat, energy, forceful interaction of elements. I'm the small figure, squeezed between the boxes, overwhelmed. The road out is available if only I can get to it! The difficulty I had was due largely to the fact that these people were *not* the cold, gray schizoid boxes. They were vibrant and alive. It was exciting to be with them. These boxes would not die "out in the cold" without me. They had their own energy. I had identified with them to the degree that *I* felt lost without *them*. Grandiosity is a constant threat to the art therapist. As we see people come alive, we are tempted to believe that we "re-created" them, like the child who reaches for the breast of his inner representation and sees it materialize. To let them go caused me to suffer once again the loneliness of isolation, to experience the separateness of my own existence.

"Memory of father" (Figure 3-2H). My father was not approachable. I admired him from a distance, fascinated as he took his chainsaw apart, expertly cleaned it, and put the pieces back together again. Sometimes there were nuts and bolts left over after the reconstruction, extra pieces for which there was no purpose. He joked about that, saying that if he saved all the pieces each time, he would eventually be able to build another chainsaw. He said it every time, and every time I laughed. He was wonderfully predictable and reliable. In actuality he was rounder than this emaciated figure. My internalized image of him is still haunted by the coldness of his funeral. My father within needs nurturing. The strong idealized self and the nurturing mother will carefully save the pieces, the spare parts, until I find a way to put them together.

My other association to this drawing is my recollection of the cookie-cutter theory. Therapy cannot be stamped out in predictable forms. There will always be leftover dough. What to do with that dough is the task of the creative therapist.

"Father at work" (Figure 3-2I). This drawing was difficult to execute. My father drove a lumber truck and was killed in a lumbering accident involving the truck. Ironically, he was being helpful at the time of the accident, intruding in a mechanical process that was not part of his job. A load of wood broke loose and crushed him. I rushed through this drawing. I was aware of wanting to get it over with. The figure inside the truck is not my father. Clearly, there is unfinished work here for me! I associate helpfulness with death. Sometimes I intrude, a function of my "chicken soup" therapist. A Gestalt therapist wrote an article with the title "Sometimes Chicken Soup Is Poison," describing the process of emasculating a patient with advice and instructions.

"Father therapist for the schizoid patient" (Figure 3-2J). The steel box is in expert hands. It is being pried open with careful, manipulative skill. The tools stand ready. Father therapist has the theoretical knowledge and the experience to take over when mother therapist's nurturing fails. In the capacity of father therapist I am objective and technical. I hammer, lubricate, examine, repair, and reorganize. I like this image. It provides a balance for me.

"Paranoid position" (Figure 3-2K). I resisted this drawing. It contains the rather stereotypical, repetitious forms I've seen executed by paranoid patients. It seems outside myself, but then my own rage is outside myself. I left out the grandiose element because my own grandiosity seems more connected to my idealized self than to the angry, kicking infant.

My response to the paranoid patient is like my response to this drawing: intellectually distancing. The paranoid fuses with my own guilt, and consequently I feel inadequate, helpless. What is needed here is some "angry kid" energy to allow some fusing, some validation, some containment for the paranoid rage.

"Therapist for the paranoid patient" (Figure 3-2L). The figure looks uninvolved, the door is open. She is the masquerading, cold witch. I stand with my arms extended to balance myself, *not* to hold the patient. In fact, I wish he'd leave through the open door! My therapeutic skills seem to be limited to providing impersonal reality testing for this whirling tornado. I'm clearly saying, "Don't get close to me!" As this impersonal figure, I'm a sitting duck for the paranoid's rage and my own. What the patient needs here is the opposite of what I feel. He needs me to stand up to his assault with righteous indignation, to provide a response unlike the ones he usually elicits. Again, the "angry kid," tempered by the "expert mechanic father," needs developing.

The art therapist is more than the classical transferential object. She must demonstrate in the therapeutic relationship her own capacity to love, hate, play, reason, hold on, and let go. In so doing, she is Winnicott's "good enough mother," making available a facilitating environment for change.

Summary Impression

As I review Pia's verbal and nonverbal communications, I become well acquainted with the angry child within her who has been assuaged with softness and tenderness. That has produced a vulnerability to regress to an oral feeding union with mother and has made Pia far more comfortable with softer, soothing affects than with bitter rage and oral spite. Confrontation and anger are not comfortable affects for Pia to utilize, making resonance with angry and aggressive states in patients difficult. Under pressure she may have trouble maintaining her boundaries and fostering a sense of separateness in her patients. This may be exacerbated by the tendency we see for her to become depleted and move to a lower energy level under stress.

That is not to say, however, that Pia is a pushover, for she clearly makes her presence felt as her representations take up space and create a well-defined statement of her ideas and moods. Furthermore, she seems to have the emotional resources to bounce back from her withdrawals and feelings of depression, and her very strong ego ideal creates an intense emotional commitment to her patients that provides a firm structure of warmth and receptivity.

A strong feminine element runs throughout Pia's representations; the male imago remains somewhat in the background. As Pia herself points out, the father within her can use more nurturing so he can be drawn on more consistently in therapy.

This student brings to her patients a wide range of intensity and affects as well as an internal structure that will permit her to resonate with some of her patients' deeper issues.

Betty Costa

"Lonely person" (Figure 3-3). X did not get lonely very often, but when she did, she viewed the world as very bland and empty. She said of this drawing: "When I leave myself [the building], I am lonely. The path in the drawing leads to other people/places, but I am still lonely." She said she enjoyed being alone, which is not being lonely. It seems that for X loneliness is a derivative of external needs. Being alone helps X to balance internal and external needs.

The drawing looks empty but not especially lonely. Blue is an internalizing color, which X used to depict herself through the symbol of the building. The building seems large enough to encompass the space and sense of self that provides X with internal strength.

Figure 3-3.

A strong phallic symbol seems to be guarding the door to the building. X said having time to be alone is a top priority in her life; she guarded her privacy and kept a close watch on her internal temperature.

"The rejected/lonely self" (Figure 3-4). X remembered feelings of rejection from her early childhood. She had felt openly rejected by both parents, which for a time left her feeling socially rejected. Her comment on the drawing was "I didn't understand why I was rejected. I think it made me very self-protective and strong."

The shapes in the drawing are very large, with sharp teeth-like shapes around the inside edges—some dripping with "tears," some with extra teeth added to other teeth, and some reinforced from the inside (self-protection)? Did she chew up the hurt and anger, swallow it, then spit it back in finding her own self-worth? The use of purple and black (passion and anger) depicted her deep feelings in this area.

The bottom shape in the drawing (tears and sharp teeth) appears intact, with a reasonable balance of inner/outer emotions. X said her feelings of rejection caused her to turn to herself for acceptance; she set her own standards of self-worth. She learned to trust herself because there was no one else.

"Leaving the Waumbek—running away during the night" (Figure 3-5). X expressed herself with simple but strong lines in this drawing. She remembered feelings of despair and how she wanted to run away from what caused it, but there was no running away for her. She said her misery stuck to her like glue. (This seems to appear in the lower right-hand corner of the drawing.) Her choice of colors was dramatic: purple, suggesting her passion and mixed emotions; red, her anger within; and black, her misery and despair.

She said, "The problem is always within me. Problems are not external; it's how I handle them. Running away is not the answer."

Possibly running away suggests to X a form of self-rejection. Thus, she introjects the problem, solves it as best she can, and creates a feeling of acceptance. Her "rejected" self seems to have formulated some of her problem-solving techniques.

"Paranoid" (Figure 3-6). In this drawing X appears very an-

Figure 3-4.

Figure 3-5.

Figure 3-6.

gry and prepared to fight, but she doesn't know what she is fighting for. She was angry at the two pairs of "empty" eyes looking at her (left side of drawing). She called them "judgmental, uncaring eyes." The eyes were drawn outside of her anger, indicating that she probably kept much of her anger to herself.

X generally didn't feel paranoid (or else she didn't recognize the feeling); therefore, it was difficult for her to define her feelings about this drawing.

Possibly the anger in the drawing grew from her early childhood rejection combined with community judgment; i.e., reject the child and then watch her fail/succeed with critical "eyes."

Summary Impression

Betty describes herself as forceful, self-directed, and highly motivated. Her identification with the strong male imago has been employed as a positive force, maintaining a mood of helpfulness and buoyancy. We see a reservoir of hurtful aggression taken in but then positively converted and used in the service of being a helpful therapist who will facilitate the social and ego skills of her patient. On the other hand, Betty is not very comfortable with the softer, more receptive parts of herself. I suspect that somewhere in her background there must have been an early grief and sadness connected to the female figure. That whole area seems less integrated within the personality, as the thrust of her energies is outward rather than inward in coping with social realities. As a result, Betty may have problems with patients with sad, depressed affects who require empathy. Not being a runner but rather a problem solver, Betty may be removed from the schizoid part of herself. Ironically, that is the world in which she lives. To use her description of herself, she is always alone even when she is with others.

Rage and anger are not unfamiliar feelings to Betty, but there is some real question as to whether she can see past her defensive anger to relate to patients' fears of fusion and softness. I suspect that she will be demanding of her patients and push them toward separateness and autonomy as was the case in her life, but she may have trouble with those individuals who may need a period of regression before they are ready to move on toward new levels of synthesis.

In short, we see a very responsible, clearly defined, and goal-oriented person who is well aware of her values and motivations.

PAIRED EXERCISE SERIES

In this section student's saw slides of their partners' drawings—"lonely," "rejected," "running away," and "paranoid" patients inside themselves.

Their task was to create a nonverbal holding environment for each of those "patients," with the understanding that that meant depicting the appropriate distance, affect, and so on that would best resonate with their "patients" and facilitate treatment. The students presented their visual responses without accompanying verbal reflections.

Betty Costa's Holding Environment for Pia Mitchel

"Lonely patient" (Figures 3-1A, 3-7A). Betty moves right into Pia's space and makes her presence felt with an image that is open and full of energy. Her strength is very much in evidence, for she is clear, structured, and fluid. In fact, she is perhaps a bit too powerful and overwhelming. Now she must work toward using her strength as a means to modulate her presence so that she can provide a softer, more soothing frame for her patient. For instance, the use of warmer colors, rather than the green previously associated by Betty with wordly experience, would have provided a more nurturing holding space here. Betty would benefit from becoming more familiar with the nurturing, lost mother in herself to make that part more available in the therapeutic process.

"Rejected patient" (Figures 3-1B, 3-7B). Once again, Betty aggressively moves into the therapeutic space with very clear, defined boundaries and movement that is purposeful and direct. A strong right hand takes the rejected patient under her wing. The energy here seems to be directed toward social mobility rather than toward healing wounds. One wonders if this well-defined activist stance will resonate with the affect of Pia's rejected patient of pale and faded colors. This patient might well need a more quiet presence with a focus on the inside rather than the outside before she can move on.

"Running away patient" (Figures 3-1D, 3-7C). Betty's passion and need for structure are very much in evidence here. Her use of purple, a color that has previously represented a deeply felt sense of emotional intensity, and her mirroring steel box seem to make the statement: "I am here, but I am separate." That clearly represents a respect for the patient's need for isolation. As important as that is, it may not entice this patient out of her frightened, withdrawn space. There are a couple of softer lines reaching out from one box to another that provide more gentleness, unity. Perhaps a greater use of curved lines would reinforce that softness while respecting the patient's need to withdraw and lick her wounds.

"Paranoid patient" (Figures 3-2K, 3-7D). As in other pictures,

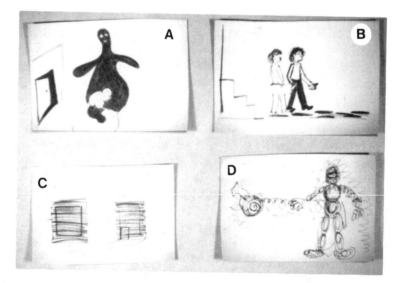

Figure 3-7.

Betty moves in with force and power. In this instance she mirrors the high energy level and engages the patient's whirlpool of fury. Betty is available for dialogue. She may find, however, that the strength of her statement may cause her paranoid patient to react defensively out of fear of being attacked. Betty needs to get past the outer defensive wall and make contact with the paranoid's wish for oneness and fusion.

In summary, Betty's identification with the male imago on both compensatory and adaptive levels provides a wellspring for both strengths and weaknesses in these four drawings. She offers her patients structure, a high energy level, and an awareness of social reality. At the same time she tends to move away from the softer, more vulnerable parts of her personality. Her further growth as a therapist and a person will be connected with her making friends with the lost female part of herself and integrating that softness with the positive and constructive forces she currently offers her patients.

Pia Mitchel's Holding Environment for Betty Costa

"Lonely patient" (Figure 3-8A). Pia's soft receptive mother is mobilized in working with Betty's lonely patient. Through the metaphor of the warm open door, she invites the patient to come in from her background of dark dysphoric emptiness. She communicates the message that she is available and present yet respects her patient's need for distance and privacy. The nonverbal message is "I understand your boxlike structure and resonate with it, yet I can offer you something different if you dare to risk being exposed and vulnerable." We see here acceptance and emotional availability for contact.

Pia must be careful of her patient's maneuvers, however. Her patient states that although there are people in her life in the end she is always alone. Consequently, there may be elements of a "false self" that compensates and defends against an inner void. The patient may need a confronting partner who will travel with her into her inner world and confront her with how available she really is to share with others.

"Rejected patient" (Figure 3-8B). Pia's response to Betty's

rejected, lonely self is a complicated one. She offers food, nurturing, and softness, and she adopts the color purple to communicate her passionate understanding of her patient's dilemma.
Pia's softness and availability may prove to be too much for her
patient to digest, however. In Pia's response we see the potential
for relatedness on a most profound level that can likewise stimulate a good deal of anxiety. Pia recognizes Betty's intense
yearning for contact with a woman, the lost mother within, but
may not be aware of her patient's accompanying fear of that.
Furthermore, in spite of her sadness, Betty has adopted a wariness of deep emotional relatedness as well as stance in life that
relies on no one but herself. The intense tenderness with sexual
overtones emanating from Pia's womblike image may simply be
too much for her patient. Pia will need to mobilize the sharpness
and clarity of her father within and become aware of the power
of her imagery if she is to provide a safe frame within which
Betty can reintegrate her lost mother.

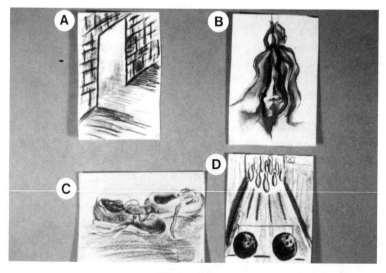

Figure 3-8.

"Running away patient" (Figure 3-8C). You may remember that Betty is not a runner, she is a problem solver. In Pia's offering her a pair of running shoes with a deep, nurturing quality, the therapist is directly confronting her patient's very adaptive defense. The message is "You don't have to be so tough and independent; sometimes running away isn't so bad." The question is, can the patient utilize this response, or is it a trifle too removed from her way of approaching the world? A better response might include hardness and toughness along with the softness and mirroring use of warm, clear colors that show a deep connectedness and an awareness of her patient's intensity. Somewhere the patient must hear the message that even tough guys can use help.

"Paranoid patient" (Figure 3-8D). Betty's paranoid patient claims that she doesn't recognize when she feels paranoid, and indeed the patient's anger seems removed from the paranoid position. Betty's two empty eyes are nearer the schizoid than the paranoid state. Pia approaches the situation with a sense of playfulness and mutuality. She converts the two empty eyes into bowling balls, and the anger seems to dissipate into a game of skill. She reaches out to her patient in the mood of energy and warmth but then loses something of the playfulness as the lack of a human image becomes apparent. Does the expression of anger throw off the therapist's sense of relatedness? Certainly, the therapist is right in choosing an aggressive game that is both safe and structured. The anger, though, is essentially a cover that defends the patient against social contact and may well need more direct confrontation than the game alone provides.

As we review Pia's four pictures, we see a warm, intuitive and receptive therapist whose weakness is being all too sensitive to the regressive pulls of her patients. Her strength and her weakness are in her connection to the soothing maternal part of herself in the treatment dialogue. In the process she may not always be ready to push her patients to individuate and gain autonomy. One wishes there were more of a father present who could lend a helping hand in problem solving and pushing things along.

Michaela Rowen's Holding Environment for Pia Mitchel

"Withdrawn patient" (Figure 3-9A). Michaela understands the territory of the schizoid's inner world and moves right into it. We see how Michaela's inner voice of loneliness makes deep, resonant contact with her patient. She is present but nonintrusive. Her nonverbal voice reaches out to say, "Open your steel box and find my warmth; feel my outstretched hands; experience

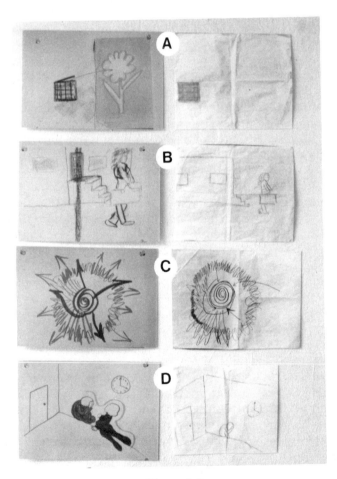

Figure 3-9.

the golden warmth that is here for you to touch." Michaela feels her patient's blackness and offers the transitional space necessary to move through blur to further definition. She challenges Pia to take a chance, while offering her strength, clarity, and softness.

Michaela's tree does seem somewhat askew and not really in harmony with her patient's black box, which leads me to suspect that there is an element of fear mixed in with her wish for contact.

"Rejected patient" (Figure 3-9B). Walking side by side with her patient, Michaela communicates the message "I am with you and present." Her drawing is sharp and defined as well as clear and aggressive. It offers hope to her patient, although there is also a sense of sadness and moroseness. Will the sharpness and clarity give further definition to her patient, and can this picture help her patient deal with rage directed outward rather than inward? Perhaps her determined, self-assertive stance would be more easily assimilated by the patient if the image contained more of a frontal view.

"Paranoid patient" (Figure 3-9C). Michaela meets her patient with vibrancy and intensity. The brilliance of the colors shooting outward seem a trifle overpowering for Pia's paranoid patient and may put her off, although there is also an inner core of unity and wholeness available. More open receptivity and fewer arrows would lessen the likelihood of provoking her patient into an angry stance. On the other hand, because anger is such a difficult affect for Pia, the successful navigation of such a defined and intense confrontation might help her patient to become better integrated.

"Lonely patient" (Figure 3-9D). Again, Michaela's familiarity with despair and hopelessness makes its presence felt. She reaches out with a symbiotic-style resonance while offering her patient separateness and empathy. The therapist gives the message that she is there and connected, as her hands are available to receive the patient. The golden line connects them, and yet there is also an opening to offer her patient the safety of retreat. Michaela offers her patient the opportunity for more definition and a mind/body relatedness that may create within her patient the courage to open up her eyes and see.

In reviewing the preceding responses and interactions a

number of points become evident. The personalities of the three students are very different, with contrasting strengths and weaknesses that will show themselves in divergent therapeutic styles. Consequently, they will help different patients in different ways at different times. That is true of all therapists: we each have our unique contribution to make as well as our own sets of limitations.

Learning theory seems to be richest when it is an emotional, cognitive, and perceptual affair. Utilizing exercises like those observed in the preceding pages takes maturity, openness, and trust. What we, and the students who so generously shared their experiences with us, have seen is the degree to which theory interfaces with the therapist's internal world to produce a therapeutic framework with unique coloration and character style. To the extent that we integrate theory with an emotional understanding of the many varieties of self and object alliances, then to that degree we will be able to be elastic in creating the appropriate holding environments for our patients.

Chapter 4

AESTHETICS OF HEALING WITHIN THE INNER REPRESENTATIONAL WORLD

Arthur Robbins
and Priscilla Rogers

In the preceding chapter we saw how the therapist tries to offer the optimal holding environment in which a patient can play with the symbols of his inner representational world. In all of the cases one or more art forms were used to mirror the energy, color, and shape of emerging themes, thus reflecting the interconnections between aesthetics and psychodynamics. The symbols of one's inner representational life are laid down early and are modified or added to in each successive developmental stage, leaving their signatures in whatever art media an individual works. That means that each personal crisis of identity can be organized within an art container that will possess a characteristic energy and structure.

This chapter presents the exploration of one advanced student as she grapples with the artist within the therapist in search of a synthesis of aesthetic and psychodynamic forms. We'll see the ongoing counterbalancing of the forces of definition and individuation versus fusion and oneness as she depicts various levels in object-related development. Priscilla Rogers and her peers in an advanced art therapy seminar were asked to create drawings and accompanying comments describing the nuances and struggles of self and other, as well as the nonverbal interplay of color, shape, shading, and energy on the following themes:

1. Depiction of myself (no guidelines).
2. The experience of deprivation whether reflected in the loss of love or in perceptions of the outside world and experiences in it.
3. A mandala of the early stages of object relations development from fusion and symbiosis through the various differentiating stages to rapprochement and object constancy.
4. The experience of an unresolved conflict.
5. The imagined somatization, or taking into the body, of the various parts of the conflict.
6. My personal conception of healing energy.

Let's let Priscilla speak for herself.

I begin with the drawing of myself (Figure 4-1A). I stand open-armed and brightly colored in a natural environment. The colors are pure and contained, though not rigidly. There is a sense of freedom, innocence, circulation, and oneness with the environment. There is also an animal-like naturalness about the connection with nature, and the yellow color fuses my body with the mountain behind. This is the first appearance of yellow as symbolic fusion. The red is flowing and discharging energetically, as though a wind were blowing. There are elements of the central yellow body, the red circulating, and the energetic quality that joins with the healing energy of the final drawing. There is a subtle interplay between the fusion and drawn boundaries in the drawing and a felt contact with a personal source of healing energy. The purple implied orb on which I am standing, a world, feels dense and mysterious in contrast to this, and I have objects at my feet that look solid and certain, black and white. Yet they are also reminiscent of children's toys. This is a paradoxical playful attitude toward what appears certain—the reality, the man-made structures of the world as opposed to nature: two sides of the external world.

This is a drawing with a wide perspective that accesses much of the feeling of childhood. If I look at this drawing as also being an expression of the child self, I see the flip side of this happy oneness with nature as a protective fusion in yellow with Great Mother Nature and a burial of the actual fusion with the mother in her giant earthiness. There is a hint of the child's fantasy of merging with a mother who does not deny or demand anything in relationship beyond youth and innocence. There is a larger-than-life quality in the self-expression, which is on the one side a healing oneness of the separate self with the universe and at the other pole a regression to features of preseparation grandiosity and security of the first year of life. Not surprisingly, yellow is a color often associated with youth and a color that very young children often prefer for its qualities of warmth and happiness.

The drawing of the experience of deprivation (Figure 4-1B)

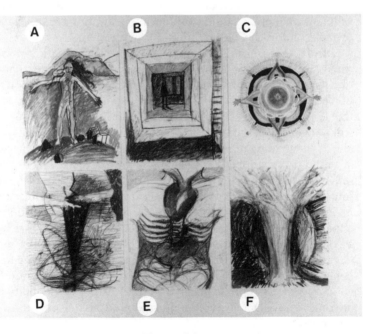

Figure 4-1.

is almost totally black and white, which stands in contrast to the first drawing. Where the compensating optimism was active in the former, here it is depleted. The depressed black figure stands facing away, withdrawn in a schizoid position into an environment of man-made buildings and endless walls. There is a sterility, a nothingness about the environment. Yet the defense against the experience of deprivation seems to serve to accentuate the boundaries between self and outside, which are clouded, vague, and senseless. It is a protective yet dead environment.

Below, along the bottom of the drawing, is a foundation of messy color; red underneath and black on top. Anger and depression become a confused emotional energy for which the structure of the white walls overcompensate. There is nothing natural here, as if what is civilizing and socializing (symbolized by the city outside) becomes a source of deprivation split off from the source that was present in the first drawing. The black and white that were contained in forms and integrated into a multidimensional environment in the first drawing have now taken over becoming the whole self and environment.

In freely associating I continue to give voice to the drawing thus: Repetitive, it is like a maze, a rat race . . . the punctuation of the corners is all I have . . . I have deified it . . . I have lived perfectly within the rules. My life is taken over by being sure that I am following them . . . that I blend in so well that no one will notice. The perpetuation of limitation to the exclusion of all else . . . a blending of schizoid reaction and depressive melancholy . . . a gnawing doubt that perhaps I am all that is black. I am only my shadow, so I cannot see my shadow. It would be too much to cast it where I could see it. It is behind and blackens me. I am engulfed, which is what I fear most, and yet I do not experience it. The depression lives beneath and is much richer. I conceptualize and think and raise myself. I am in my most deprived position, for I am furthest away from self and the most believing of my own false self-construction. I am desperate for contact, and yet there is no such thing. It is not a possibility for anyone, really. Deprivation is more than a private truth: it is a truth about the world.

Like Winnicott's (1971) expositions on the construction of a "false self," this position, with its complex schizoid and depressive features, carries also the features of the protective creation of a mask self constructed around an idealized, perfected, self-image that replaces a vulnerable, partially unrelated, perhaps unintegrated and felt-as-unworthy true self. The mask self can function well in the world until the demands of reality for the relatedness and intimacy threaten to uncover its fraudulent nature, and it must withdraw to avoid confronting any unworthiness and helplessness underneath. Retreating into grandiosity is the lone possibility, an escape to that place where one can again be king of the world, reminiscent of that early developmental period before about eight months of age, where the infant is in this position vis-à-vis the world.

In this position, everything coming from the outside is seen as an intrusion. As Horner (1979) writes about the construction of the false self, it is originally constructed as a response to early feelings of the mother as intrusive. Life becomes a series of reactions to intrusion. "Identity becomes consolidated around the reactive stance vis-à-vis the object." The self is "reacting to the environment rather than generating and initiating his own spontaneous and goal-directed behavior" (p. 174).

As what is bad is projected outward and self is identified as special and good (in the schizoid type of defense), energy is expended in patrolling the division and re-creating a rigid division between those two realms to gain a sense of boundary. Actually, the felt sense of boundary is very cloudy. The elements of watching, patrolling, fearing punishment, persecution, and intrusion point to Melanie Klein's original linking of the schizoid with the paranoid position. However, often the compensatory preoccupation with creating a powerful false self-image with great functional ability, and a concomitant retreat into a predifferentiated grandiosity, overrides any conscious awareness of the paranoid features.

When reality impinges on this deprived self and forces it to attempt relationship, the observing and watchful qualities return as a regressive checking back reminiscent of the practicing period. In acting out this position of deprivation in the drawing, there are so few bearings in the real world that that which has replaced the object, the private world, must be preserved and returned to often, until any straying too far is dangerous.

At the core there is resentment of this leash, which is really the uncut cord to the mother. If a mother continues in various ways to be unsupportive of the separation and individuation of the child, defenses grow in complexity, especially as the infant approaches the crisis of rapprochement. This deep defensive posture is counterbalanced by the open, warm, happy posture and also real possibility seen in the first drawing (Figure 4-1A).

The first two drawings introduce the innocent, youthful, fused, at-one-with-nature self-image, partly embodying the open, warm qualities of a true inner core, and also elements of an optimistic, constructive mask. The figure is spontaneous and colorful; it seems to have some contact with its creative source in the first drawing, although remaining alone. The defensive self, in deprivation, denied the fusion allowable in the first drawing, creates detachment many times over. It mourns the absence of Mother Nature, and remains alone. Neither expression of independence and aloneness is an effective separation and individuation. Undisguised fusion is a deep threat to the individuating self. It is experienced as engulfing, intruding, and denying of self, like an intrusive mother who will not allow a child to separate and discourages any steps toward autonomy (Figure 4-1C).

The mandala was created next by choosing elements, symbols, and colors from my own inner experience of the stages of growth from oneness to separateness. It is built outward with the early stages in the center. It is a highly organized and balanced piece, with a wide range of color, imagery, and texture synthesizing many disparate inner elements and pointing to a high level of ego functioning. The strong balance helps to keep together my sense of self as I deal with strongly charged material and memories, feelings and images. Many of the same colors and images occur as in the first drawings. Notably, the yellow appears in the mandala as associated with fusion, as it was in the first drawing (Figure 4-1A). Here the fusion experience is synthesized within the whole self. The painful part of the experience of separation shows up as portions of black and white again and is synthesized and ordered within a centered structure. The piece is compartmentalized and intellectually designed to a certain extent. Intellectualization defends against the charge of the material and also serves to integrate polarities and create a way to experience a sense of the whole.

As I reflect on the mandala, I let myself write what lives for me in some of its images. In the mandala I seek a solution for polarizing conflicts. I go past the experiences of the here and now and integrate my circumstances in the circle, which is the totality where everything comes into resolution. The yellow of fusion is both within and protected at its source, while also being brought forth in the outer circle where its lumination offers opportunity for fusion with sources of imaginal power. Here the energy that has radiated from the center manifests itself in the varied symbolic representations on the outskirts of the wheel.

There is the circle of the empty mouth and the circle of the fulfillment of all things beyond satisfaction. The fear of the yellow is that of attachment by the organism to satisfaction and the binding of the self to the empty mouth—to the psychology of need, desire, and scarcity. (Notice also that the yellow is missing from the drawing of "conflict" and in the "somatization of the conflict.")

The blackness has become a gate. The mandala offers an opportunity to rest in the paradoxical realities between the black and white, between the positive and negative experiences echoing our original oneness and separateness, our paradise and our fall, our original love and comfort, and our desperation that lives as alienation and isolation from all we cease to allow, all we cease even to envision. The mandala offers an opportunity to envision, to begin to create a perspective that can hold paradoxes and resolve the binding of the self. The experience of the black and white becomes a gate into the yellow—the yellow as a triangle, now given form. Fusion and form unite and heal.

The fusion section of the mandala is the serpentine, twisting yellow portion. It is the two entwined, the beginning of rhythm. The orange fusion was the original color at the center and is the most difficult to return to. The orange is sought again in the rainbow, but it does not lead to expansion. It is still the fusion with nature. There are definite paths to the outer circle, to expansion, to the power of the imagination. The activity of creating a mandala in a circle is an approach to the self in its own first image. Yet the mandala on the outside circle is very much like a clock, indicating a strange mixture of the pacing of time and the stillness of the elements, the permanence and persistence of the circle in the march of time.

The creation of the mandala enlarges the view of life to a holistic one and is felt as a walking away from feeling inundated by experience, the victim of circumstance. I become responsible for the design, the completion, and the carrying outward of all aspects of my earliest experience. At the same time this is an inclusion of responsibility for life, and I find the urge to beautify, to see selectively, to manipulate and control by the ego. The rawness and energy of the first drawing is missing in this, a bird's-eye view of the whole. The mandala makes the rawness workable. This is a resting place. I rest often in the intellect and reach to integrate wide polarities.

Recognizing now in the drawings the remaining ties to the state of fusion, I can better understand my own defenses of intellectualization and pursuits of self-sufficiency in terms of Blanck and Blanck's "unevenness in development characterized by pseudo self-sufficiency in which part of the ego replaces the symbiotic partner" (Horner, 1979, p. 211). The tragic themes that often enter into my artwork indicate my association on a deep level of my pursuit of art with early object loss. In line with what has been presented thus far, for much of my life my talent lived in a rarefied atmosphere, where it could not be contaminated or intruded on. I created a symbiotic partner in my work and protected it from ever leaving.

Coming to a climax at about the age of eighteen months, at the stage of rapprochement, was my mother's inability to allow me to stand, to aggress, to gain autonomy because of her own narcissistic needs. Though devoted, she brought with her her own depressive defenses and was often physically ill or absent. She needed me to live out what she could not bring to fruition in herself. Early on, when it was most needed, there were times when support failed, as there are in every family. Her absence, however, physical or otherwise, signaled my turning to the intellect and to solitary pursuits as substitute objects.

To the extent to which I enroll others into becoming partners in relationships from which I cannot differentiate to some degree, and from which I must distance parts of myself when deprived of approval and love, I also cut off here-and-now contact, preventing the creation of transitional, alive space. Thus, there is always the need to risk stepping out of the seeming comfort of the defended, detached posture. This nearly always puts me in contact with the helplessness, dependency, loss of support, omnipotence, and illusory power with which I create my high-functioning adult self, a pathological entity that this society idealizes highly. As I notice those issues that have their origin, at least in part, in the rapprochement stage, I remember that I was hospitalized and necessarily separated from my parents for 4 to 6 weeks with pneumonia when I was eighteen months old. The issues that appear in the drawings confirm difficulties with the developmental tasks of this stage.

"At the beginning of the rapprochement period the child begins to widen his world, extending it to include others besides his mother" (Horner, 1979, p. 121). Conflicts arise when the part of me that has not resolved this developmental stage prevents my circle from widening beyond either my original partnership, often represented as a partnership with my work or intellect, or beyond the creation of a private orbit with another individual. The conflict drawing (Figure 4-1D) demonstrates the collision involved when another person enters my world who offers to participate in a symbiotic orbit, hooking into the most unresolved portions of myself, and also brings personal needs, concerns, and desires for life outside that orbit. The pattern becomes one of creation of dependency coupled with an emotional abandonment, or fears of abandonment, by the object.

In this drawing there is no space, no silence. There is a white noise reflecting the experience of fearing the fusion with another and at the same time a yearning for it. The fear has pushed the yellow fusion out of the picture. The foundations of need and dependency present are unconscious, and for that reason, are experienced as unresolvable. There is a vague feeling of wanting, but it is intellectualized, and there is evidence for abandonment. The truth of the ripping apart of a symbiotic agreement is unconscious. Only the pain of it is present.

Conflict is experienced as confusing, unbalanced, violent, and central. The indication that two people are involved is depicted in the two hands that reach toward and still reject the central space of the black funnel, the jagged and blind entry into a cyclone of movement and noise. The dramatization of the conflict, the noise, can perhaps drown or discharge the pain. I am heading for the black for direction, and the only direction is down where there is some circulation. However, a deceptive orbit of energy (the image of the entrapping symbiosis) lies at the bottom like a snare. There is a feeling that the hands are being burned and scraped by their contact with the red. There is an overwhelming sense of finality about the painful red. It is impossible to get away from it, like blood on the hands perhaps or like a guilt on a deep level for being unable to participate, for having killed a portion of the self. There is no out. This is indelible. Nothing exists outside this conflict except a designed contour that does not offer a convincing alternative—almost a laughable cartoon line without life, lying nowhere near the energy of the lines depicting the conflict, the lines of the black, the negative, the passionate, the bonded and entrapped. Inescapable repetition . . . impossibility of creation . . . unbridled expansion, whirling, engulfing motion but no expansion into silence. There is only this thing, the reality of this conflict. Any attempt to eliminate it at the bottom of the page is forbidden. A cage is drawn. There is a holding to the concept of what this relationship must be for myself to survive, and at the stage of conflict there is little ability to allow the relationship to express itself beyond the bonds of attachment.

When I take this conflict into the body in the fifth drawing (Figure 4-1E), it is calmed and contained with the intensity localized in the heart that is expanded beyond capacity. It is unable to circulate and appears almost to choke the figure. The yellow is still missing, a denial of fusion in the process of somatization of the conflict. When a conflict is manifested as a physical illness, it again becomes a way of withdrawing. When I am ill, I am taken away from the world, and "there is a sense that others cannot be approached or appealed to, which is the natural outgrowth of the rapprochement period" (Horner, 1979, p. 122). Illness more acceptably echoes the helplessness and loss of power which must erupt from time to time as the core of a conflict. Uncontained by the body, that helplessness would lead to a clouding of the organized self-representation and a feeling of the self-boundaries being incomplete. The physical body serves as a clear boundary.

Horner (1979) writes of the need to patrol the boundaries and to deny the fusion leading to anger at the truth that one has not differentiated from the chaos, merely captured it. Anorexia, from which I suffered as an adolescent (adolescence being a period that repeats many of the developmental tasks of rapprochement on another level), can be understood in light of this need to patrol boundaries, to find some control, and to deny the conflict of dependency coupled with abandonment.

There is a unilateral transfer of the content of the conflict into the body, though the affect has been flattened. The heart holds the most color, with the rest of the body taking on the conflict by nearly shutting down. Black becomes a primary color throughout but especially in the chest area. The blue of the stomach area is cool and calm, perhaps an indication of the wish to return to the comfort of a full stomach, to the state of taking in without having to give out.

As the somatization is centered in the heart, I acknowledge my core conflict. I approach the healing of the heart as a temporary and recurrent unwillingness to know with the heart, to risk circulation, to give out and trust in the return of love. Yellow is the warmth and luminosity of the sun, the great heart of the world. The healing will come with the acceptance and realization of the heart as the organ of contact with universal love. The yellow fusion is the source of circulation of personal love, along with the ability to allow states of fusion with another as a part of the natural rhythm of a relationship.

Thus far, the drawings have shown varying degrees of integration of the yellow, from the early spontaneous, through naive, creative fusion with nature, to the intellectual awareness and synthesis of the mandala, into the exclusion of the threatening fusion in the extremely deprived and conflicted states. It is difficult to risk the journey into the final drawing (Figure 4-1F) because in order to touch the yellow with its inherent power and radiance in the final healing drawing, I must be present to the blackness of this drawing also. I am close to my heartfelt eclipse, the darkening of the sun. This follows the old paths of the heart along the abandonments of my history, the scarred passions and witheld renunciations of my own autonomy. The beauty of the creative self's comment on its own healing comes in noticing that the heart and the sun are one path. "The way up is the way down," as Eliot wrote in the *Quartets*. The healing drawing compositionally is the inverse of the conflict drawing, only in the healing drawing there appears to be a limitless source of light in the central funnel.

The path with a heart is the path of the heart, also the way of greatest conflict for me. To know the healing energy of the final drawing I must be with all of this and put my hand out. I must allow the fear that comes from allowing the fusion along with the luminosity as it engulfs the boundaries of the hand and blanches its solid substance. The luminosity also energizes its circulation, releasing an infinite source of power, meant not for domination but for magnificence.

The healing will come only when I can see the pathology as a door into this space. I must risk the stance of believing that the limitations of defensive structure are not the entire truth about either self or world. I must risk what I feel my survival depends on to touch a source within which survival is not even an issue, all the while paradoxically touching it while present in the eclipse. The inclusiveness of everything erases the possibility of the oblivion that dwelled in the deprivation drawing.

After the exercises were complete, Priscilla and I proceeded to review her drawings. Both of us were aware of the importance of the color yellow and its symbolic representation of healing energy. Her comments on fusion energy being transformed into an affirmation of the self seemed especially apt. As we trace the color yellow, first it is a holding frame of a nature that both affirms and releases the self. Then it becomes completely lost in the second drawing of deprivation. Thus, as we witness the self being both protected and imprisoned by formidable walls of black and white protection, the life and expansive energy of the self dims into the distance.

In the mandala (Figure 4-1C) we again see the yellow as an important unifying force of the self, a force that is controlled yet available through the intellect, where the student allows herself to become accessible and available to the world.

In her conflict drawing (Figure 4-1D) there is again an absence of yellow as we see a divergence of the forces and tensions of pain, agitation, depression, and rage. They both oppose one another and form a cohesive integration. Perhaps we are seeing another level of healing entering the personality through the aesthetic organization. Here, although we see none of the golden yellow that uplifts or expands the personality, we do see a drawing that has power, motion, and integration. Perhaps another level of healing can move into consciousness through an expanding tolerance for a wide range of affects. Involved in this conflict drawing is a diminishing of the intellectual defenses, allowing more fluidity of form while still containing strife. By contrast, in the somatization drawing (Figure 4-1E) the large red heart seems superimposed on the drawing rather than integrated with the forces of black, purple, and blue. Again there is an absence of the color yellow.

Finally, in Priscilla's representation of healing energy (Figure 4-1F), gold expands the self upward and outward while black provides a frame in which the self can experience its boundaries. Of note, the black does not seem to be quite integrated within the drawing and seems somewhat heavy and overbalanced, indicating that the drive for wholeness and oneness with the world is not quite realizable.

In these drawings the presence or absence of gold and yellow becomes a pivotal issue for personal organization. Through golden yellows we observe warmth and the healing energies of love contacting the deepest core of the personality, an energy that expands the self into a dual level of consciousness incorporating self and the world. When we observe the color yellow in its healing form, rather than as a change in personality structure, we see it temporarily allowing Priscilla to surmount pathology for a new form of unity.

The aesthetics of healing, then, are contrasted within two different approaches to health. On the one hand, through the conflict drawing we see the personality expand through a consciousness of pain, rage, and loss to find an integration. By contrast, the healing drawing contains and overcomes that internal strife, and for a moment the color gold dominates the personality.

Let us observe the play of colors that are given somewhat

less emphasis in Priscilla's comments about her work. Central to her aesthetic expression of self are the colors red and black. In the first drawing (Figure 4-1A) the black formless toys offer an anchor to the purple grounding that gives a balance to her expansive need to cross boundaries and be at one with all others.

The dripping red color in the body image of Figure 4-1A moves into an enormous struggle with the black angry part of herself that is neatly boxed and disassociated from the center of the self. In her deprivation drawing (Figure 4-1B) the reds and blacks create a formless mass that are disassociated from the impact of the entire drawing. The self is encased with strict lines and tight controls, but in contrast to Priscilla's observation, I see the self preserved and protected from the black despair as she secretly looks out of her windows deep within her consciousness. The blacks will never destroy this woman, for there are formidable defenses that protect the self.

As we turn now to the mandala (Figure 4-1C), we observe the color yellow moving in and out of compartmentalized and intellectual defenses reflected in the circles within circles and the neat balance of color, form, and shape, Priscilla seems available and accessible to the world in spite of her strong need to balance and integrate all of the forces of her development. Perhaps the mandala form exerts too much pressure for wholeness and creates an artificial pressure toward integration that the artist is not quite ready to master. The black areas are converted into tight forms and firm barriers. Arms, however, reach out and allow people in, providing they can respect the various defenses and controls.

In the conflict drawing (Figure 4-1D) we see the symbolization of reds and blacks in dynamic conflict, an expansion of the self through dynamic lines and intense energy. Life and death are not contained but move and blur into one another. There are forces pressing in with black rage against the need for life and vitality, as expressed through the color red. Priscilla gives full play to both hate and love as manifested in the colors red and black, and she grounds, once again, the interplay of forces through the elegance and regality of the color purple.

When we return to Figure 4-1E, the red part seems unintegrated and lacking cohesion with the rest of the material. The black body seems very powerful and ominous, but indeed the heart seems stuck on and unable to offer life to the organs.

When we both returned to the healing drawing (Figure 4-1F), we were aware that the black still needed further integration with the golden warm colors of Priscilla's personality. The split of hate and love creeps out in spite of her enormous will to be expansive and whole.

If we are to contrast open and closed systems, the deprivation and somatization drawings appear fairly protected and inaccessible. On the other hand, there is much movement and availability in the conflict drawing, with its multiple levels and dimensions reflecting endless possibilities and potentialities to both viewer and artist.

Priscilla's use of shading reflects a sensitive engagement with the world and its nuances and appears to be one of her strongest pathways into expression of her life force. As intellectual controls intensify, as in the mandala drawing, her sense of texture and touch diminish into fine tight lines.

Priscilla's aesthetic overview of self and other gives an interesting insight into the source of personal power. Through the color yellow, she allows herself to bypass pathology and transcend the personal boundaries of self and other. That power may well characterize her relationship to the universe. There is another view of power in her drawings, as we see an expanded capacity to tolerate the conflict and pain that provides the self with life forces and opportunities. Here power stems from an inner strength to grapple with one's personal history, so that oppressive structures can be converted into acts of self-affirmation rather than prisons for the self.

Chapter 5

MATERIALS AS AN EXTENSION OF THE HOLDING ENVIRONMENT

Arthur Robbins
and Donna Goffia-Girasek, M.S.

Although there are inherent qualities in any given art material that may make it more or less appropriate for use with any given diagnostic category, art materials can be used in a multitude of ways to promote an ever adapting holding environment sensitive to a patient's changing levels of ego integration, defenses, resistances, object representations, and the like. This adds a subtle dimensionality to a subject that is often treated as a series of recipes for various patient populations.

From this enlarged perspective, the wide range of clinical considerations can make the choice of materials seem overwhelming. It is here that hands-on experience and personal exploration of the interface between psychodynamics and aesthetic principles can make a critical difference in a therapist's facility in utilizing art materials to enhance therapeutic communication. Materials are an organic part of theory, technique, and the processes of creativity development and therapeutic change. Experience using a wide range of media is what will give the therapist a subjective awareness of the potentialities of various materials, allowing him to capitalize on their inherent qualities as well as more creative or subtle applications to address the therapeutic issues at hand. Materials utilized in this way are clearly serving a number of functions simultaneously.

The product created from any given materials is part and parcel of the process of reorganizing a patient's perceptual field both psychologically and aesthetically. To repeat what I've discussed in other contexts as one of the most basic premises of utilizing the artist in the therapist: Everything that goes on in the therapeutic process has its aesthetic counterpart, as product and process merge to create a developmental statement of self integrating past and present. This chapter will attempt to take the psychology of art materials found in *Creative Art Therapy* (Robbins & Sibley, 1976) and integrate it with the conceptual framework of object relations therapy.

Materials can be analyzed along the dimensions of: form, texture, color, volume, space, movement, balance, and abstraction (Robbins & Sibley, 1976). Although these parameters are, in practice, intricately interrelated, the following descriptive definitions are meant to serve as the aesthetic building blocks from which more complex constructions and relationships will spring.

> *Form:* The visual image by which the subjective and objective essence of a particular subject is presented.
>
> *Texture:* The tactile quality of any given art subject.
>
> *Color:* The presence of chromatic material.
>
> *Volume:* The level of three-dimensional expression.
>
> *Space:* The volume, expansiveness, density of a particular image in relationship to its surround.
>
> *Movement:* Both the quality of kinesthetic tension associated with a particular image and the degree of muscular involvement necessary to produce it.
>
> *Balance:* The degree to which other elements such as space, color, shape are integrated.
>
> *Abstraction:* The metaphoric, symbolic, nonrepresentational depiction of reality.

These elements describe not only the dimensions of materials but also the nonverbal aspects of the internal representational life that so influences relationships between people in and out of the therapy environment. Verbal expressions abound incorporating the above aesthetic elements: expressions referring to a colorful personality; depth and breadth (volume) of character; flatness or depth of affect; the texture, form, or balance of someone's life or relationships. Likewise, a person may flood or control his communications with others or create a quality of flatness or depth in his symbolic connection with the world. Here, psychological and aesthetic principles merge to shape and organize verbal and nonverbal communications pertaining to subjective and objective reality.

FORM

When we as therapists assess the *form* of our patients' communications, we are looking at how they take the opportunity to merge subjective and objective perception to present their views of internal and external reality. Representations may be overly stilted and concrete, suggesting a rigid and/or narrow view of reality, with an accompanying rigid defense system and ego structure. On the other hand, the form may go beyond all boundaries of consensual reality to offer an excessively subjective and egocentric sense of existence.

There is also a very real correlation between ego functioning and aesthetic form. As we observe more difficulties in patients who have problems in ego functioning, there is an accompanying deterioration in aesthetic form. All of the elements of space, movement, image, form become fragmented and lack cohesiveness. As a patient gains more self-definition or structure and his observing ego develops, the art form produced likewise shows more definition and dimensionality. Materials become the stuff with which the patients structure and share their perceptions and inner life—quite literally, give them form.

TEXTURE

Being aware of the qualities of *texture* associated with various materials is important from the perspective of the touch issues of any given patient. On one level those issues have to do with one's style of relating to others, as seen projected into the "texture" of the therapeutic relationship. To say someone reacts with softness, roughness, or sharpness is not simply a figure of speech. Those words bring to mind images of people we know. Materials can be used to mirror, complement, or confront such dimensions. For instance, materials like clay, plastilene, stuffed forms, play dough have a soft quality; materials like stone, plaster, wood, metal are hard and brittle; printing inks and oil-based paints are sticky.

In addition to considering object-relatedness it would behoove the therapist to look at the ego level of the patient in question. For instance, a patient on a presymbiotic level is in need of materials that provide soothing, comforting sensations in order to encourage libidinal development. Soft, furry, warm textures would clearly be more appropriate than, say, sandpaper or armature wire. It might become important to use different textures with an autistic child, or actually stroke him, to help shift the focus from proprioceptive workings to a cathection of the external body.

Subtle variations exist in very similar materials. Think of the difference in stimulation between terra cotta and porcelain clay, for example. Whereas the former is basic, primitive, gritty, the latter seems more pristine in its smooth whiteness. Using those two forms of clay, the therapist might confront or complement issues associated with their inherent qualities.

Now consider plaster, with its inherent transition from warm, soft, and flowing liquid to cool, well-defined hardness. Its transitory nature might be played with in instances where the issue of separation–individuation involving the evolution of self–object differentiation and definition predominate. Sensitivity on the part of the therapist is critical here because patients might experience that kind of play as either threatening or releasing. The same patient who finds the speed of the transition in plaster too frightening could conceivably find a slow-drying clay an easier medium with which to work.

COLOR

Color makes a visual statement that describes a patient's state of being. The ultimate criteria for assessing the patient's choice are the subjectively felt experience the color communicates, along with the associations of the patient to it. Caution must be taken by the therapist to remain objective in his assessment of the patient's use of color, for his own cultural and personal biases may cause a subjective reaction to particular selections of hue and chroma. For instance, Jung states that colors may be attributed to the four functions of perception and judgment: green for sensation, yellow for intuition, red for feeling, blue for thinking. Throughout history, however, various cultures have developed their own schemas, such as red for the hunt, violence, harvest, and green for abundance. The therapist can play with some of those notions but cannot dogmatically apply formulas. Red might, in fact, represent violence or warmth; blue, coldness or regality; yellow, energy or tumultuousness; purple, soothing or seduction; white, a void or synthesis of all colors. We must use our artistic and aesthetic as well as our therapeutic sensibilities to understand fully, to recognize, and to accept our patients' views of their realities through the colors they choose.

If, in fact, patients choose colors that express their current emotional states, we as therapists can suggest other colors to create a dialogue in contrasts and alternatives. One example might be the individual who denies blackness by the excessive use of white space. He might ultimately need to explore dark chromatic places in art expression. Likewise, a preoccupation with dark, heavy affects might require the contrasting vitality of yellow or orange. The cold rationality of blues may contrast and counter the spontaneous, childlike expression of pinks or reds. The therapist attempts to integrate polarities and splits within the psychic organization that are expressed through color and that ultimately parallel and metaphorically describe the affective states of the patient's internal representations.

Color is most obviously associated with such materials as tempera, watercolors, oil paints, color pencils, crayons, cray-pas, chalks, and pastels. All of these materials have intrinsic qualities that render them more or less appropriate at various stages of therapy and with different developmental issues. Tempera on paper is a two-dimensional expression and a primary approach, whereas watercolor and oils require more complex layering. Moving from flatness to layering of paints can metaphorically express new levels of identity synthesis on the part of a patient.

It becomes more complicated, however. Watercolor, with its unpredictability and transparent nature, is hard to control and necessitates a willingness to be spontaneous, accept change, relinquish omnipotence. Being faced with issues of control and mess can bring to the surface conflicts of disorder and shame associated with internal objects. The more positive aspects elicit discovery, creation, stimulation. Clearly, the patient with shaky boundaries, like the psychotic or the borderline in the early stages of treatment, would find watercolor a frightening medium with which to cope. Use of that medium with a depressive patient would have to be carefully assessed to determine whether it would facilitate release and needed regression or would further intensify feelings of powerlessness and impotence.

Oils offer a more predetermined and exacting challenge because the paint takes weeks to set and dry, but it also offers the patient the opportunity to make changes before the images become permanent. Patience is built into the process. The thick, creamy consistency of the oils contains substance and volume that can be built up, thinned down, or textured to resonate with a patient's needs in constructing a sense of self. There are very few materials indeed that offer the range of possibilities that include building or subtracting while playing with texture and color.

Those patients who require a gradual buildup of frustration tolerance, particularly those who are borderline, may ultimately find watercolor or oil a valuable challenge. The therapist must be aware, however, that such experiences can be offered only on a step-by-step basis as the patient gains mastery and awareness.

Colored drawing materials also offer a wide range of control, with colored pencils at one extreme and chalks at the other. Use of pencil and paper can be soothing in its ease of control, its structure, and its firm boundaries. Crayons and Magic Markers offer slightly less definition and have more permanence, lacking the pencil's quality of being erasable.

Cray-pas begin to move in the direction of more fluidity and offer an intermediate material between crayons and pastels or chalks. Once we hit these last two materials, we are dealing with lack of precision and an ever-changing pattern or image, but there is also the possibility for playing with a shifting background—qualities which could either free or frustrate the artist, depending on ego and boundary strength.

VOLUME

The importance of utilizing materials that have *volume,* or three-dimensional qualities, lies in their potential for building, subtracting, layering—the very components that go into creating representations of self and object. A therapist gets a picture of the dimensionality of his patients' object representations in terms of their flat, one-dimensional quality, such as need gratification, or of their multilevel complexity that bespeaks a rich inner life.

Materials like metal, stone, wood, plaster, clay, wax, or armature wire all have intrinsic qualities of volume that can be valuable in exploring and building adequate representations of self and other, but consider the metaphorical implications of those materials. Clay and wax can both be added or subtracted, so mistakes can be repaired, decisions can be reversed. Stone, wood, and plaster, on the other hand, basically involve taking away, so there is greater risk involved. Depending on whether the therapist wanted to mirror, complement, or confront the patient, the use of one or the other of these two groups of materials might be indicated.

Other considerations come into play. Patients struggling to assimilate powerful internal representations might use stone as a means to work through conflicts. Stone requires strength and a force of precision but does not always respond predictably to pressure. It must be respected for its own internal harmony and movement, its mysterious desire to yield to the force of nature, and its external appearance of solidity, which may stand in direct contrast to its potentially fragile and fragmented interior. It's not much of a reach to see how manipulating the divergent properties of stone could reactivate issues of separation–individuation, frustration, aggression, dominance, submission, or needs for containment associated with a patient's parental imagos.

Stone offers a particularly apt picture of how working through the aesthetic and psychodynamic challenges associated with a material can be used for developmental synthesis. With each new development of the stone, there is a loss, reorganization, and accommodation. Involved is a constant emotional and aesthetic challenge both to respect the rhythm and flow of the stone and to bring something of the individual artist to the concrete, visual statement of self and other being created.

Woodcarving has some of the same rhythm requirements as stone, and like any subtractive practice, it demands taking risks, decision making, giving up omnipotence, and being flexible. Those are qualities suggestive of patients in the throes of working through practicing or rapprochement. The internal properties of wood may be flexible and yielding or brittle and rough. Splinters fragment off the woodblock, leaving a coarse surface to be restored with sandpaper and oil to a soothing, sensuously smooth, polished form. In contrast to stone, wood has a grain and texture that provide structure, focus, and direction.

Metalwork can be used as well to explore the issues of self–object representation, but the means of joining pieces should be geared to the libidinal integration level of the patient. Welding involves the use of torch and flame, turning a cold, strong, weighty material into a dancing molten liquid yearning for direction and reorganization. The transformation can cause a tremendous sense of libidinal excitement that can simply be too much for the patient whose differentiation between self and other is primitive, whose affects are chaotic, and whose drives have not been neutralized or invested in highly organized and integrated self-systems. In such cases bolting, riveting, and dovetailing provide alternate means of construction.

Space

Regardless of the medium or the project, *space* comes into play in terms of both the space, or framework, within which to work and the patient's use of given space. A person's relationship to space begins very early, with fusion and the gradual separation, differentiation, and individuation that in a psychological sense puts space between infant and mother. Numerous issues come into play regarding firmness of ego boundaries and degree of object constancy. Some media, such as sandbox play, provide well-defined boundaries and structure, whereas others are flexible, or fluid, like charcoal or watercolors. The former can provide an environment where the patient can feel safe from the swallowing introjects of his internal world and can offer firm boundaries in which to explore the relationships between internal and external reality.

Watercolor, as has been noted before, runs all over the wet space that is provided, potentially causing a great deal of anxiety to the person with loose ego boundaries or fear of fusion.

Clearly, the optimal space a patient is given in which to work must be gauged individually. Consider the difference between being faced with putting an image on a small piece of paper, a large piece of paper, or a mural tacked to the wall. The lack of containment, and potentially the sense of being overwhelmed, becomes increasingly greater as the work space to be handled grows.

Now let's add the additional element of moving out into space, such as in Elaine Rapp's technique (Robbins & Sibley, 1976, p. 226) in which the patient is required to throw, catch, and swirl tissue paper to music. The body, materials, and movement intertwine fluidly to expand and shape space. Venturing into the undefined world of fluid space requires the strong internal anchor of object constancy and should not be attempted with patients in danger of ego diffusion.

Finally, how a patient uses space offers a lead-in to numerous issues. Does the patient's artwork make a strong statement, taking up considerable space, or use small bits of space? Does the image expand, reach out, enclose, protect; have substantial density or a diffuse quality; interface with its surround in a receptive or defensive way? Again, depending on whether the therapist wants to support, mirror, or confront determines how he will structure an art experience.

Movement

Movement, rhythm, psychomotor expression become related to space when considered in terms of the varied use of one's musculature. Such issues as containment, degree of stimulation, need for release of aggressive energy, actual fine and gross motor skills also should be weighed in choosing materials.

On a most basic level, art experiences like crocheting, jewelry making, and drawing require fine motor control, whereas such activities as hammering and chopping require more gross motor skill. As fine and gross motor skills connect with developmental issues, some patients need the structure, control, and sense of mastery of repetitive fine motor activities. Stitchery, weaving, knotting fibers, stringing beads, in addition to the fine motor activities mentioned above, offer such containment. Containment also can come from using materials in a way that reduces the stimulation level or limits movement, like collage with a selection of materials predetermined by the therapist or use of crayons or pencils on paper carefully selected for size. Containment is especially appropriate for patients with a psychotic organization, whose boundaries are already too fluid or who experience their environments as manipulative or chaotic.

Some patients may retreat into the use of such materials or repetitive activities as a defensive maneuver, and they might, over time, need to be moved into more gross motor activities if the therapeutic process is to be kept from going stagnant.

Other patients, especially those dealing with contained rage associated with early self–object relations, can benefit from large-muscle activities and more aggressive use of materials. Use of materials involving hammering, sawing, chopping, chiseling, or tearing most obviously come to mind, but there are also activities, such as papermaking, cast paper, and the various forms of printing, that lend themselves to that sort of release. Again, the degree of object constancy should be assessed because printing calls for the ability to abstract and exhibit continuity, skills not acquired at early developmental levels. Printing also can be useful in building frustration tolerance and encouraging exploration and discovery because the artist must learn to capitalize on mistakes and accidents to find new avenues of expression.

ABSTRACTION

The ability to *abstract* is closely related to symbol formation, a function that does not appear developmentally until rapprochement. That is the phase in which the child must give up his delusions of grandeur and accept true separateness from mother. It is the development of language, the internalization of a "good mother" and rules/demands, and the ability to express wishes and fantasies through symbolic play that facilitate the process. Once acquired, the use of symbols can either act as an organizing factor to synthesize multiple levels of consciousness and one's identity, or it can become a haven in which to distract the outsider from gaining access to the true self.

It would seem obvious that the degree of abstraction asked of any given patient should reflect developmental level because requiring too great a degree of symbolization can put a great strain on ego-synthesizing capacities. As has been mentioned in relation to other aesthetic elements, psychotics need concrete and specific experiences that are task-oriented. The autistic child, at an earlier, presymbiotic level, can tolerate even fewer demands on the ability to abstract. Indeed, the materials used by autistic children must possess kinesthetic, visual, perhaps olfactory appeal. Materials are felt, pushed, pulled, squeezed in the interest of encouraging and supporting preoperational abilities (Piaget, 1936).

Borderline patients, with their conflicts in the rapprochement developmental phase, have the ability to use symbols, but they have not adequately integrated those symbols and images into greater wholes. For those patients one of the major tasks is to mend such bipolar splits as good and bad, love and hate, grandiosity and inadequacy. Before they can do so, however, they must play with their images and own them.

Any number of materials lend themselves to fantasy play, including miniature figures of people, animals, villages; dolls, puppets, masks; cardboard boxes and construction paper (any materials one can build with); shrines and shields/armor. Such materials used in fantasy play can represent many facets of the self, including ego, id, and superego. They can be used to redefine early symbiosis or serve as transitional objects. They also can help in defining and reclaiming lost objects, in completing unfinished business, and in gaining a deeper understanding and integration of the forces and internalizations that make us all who we are.

Using materials in an integrated way with object relations principles becomes an art in itself. Through a developing sense of mastery and familiarity with art materials, an ever-growing repertoire of themes, and a firm developmental grounding, the therapist can determine appropriate usage with a given population or patient. Without them his presentation of experiences and options to patients is merely intuitive, nonspecific, and unguided. Because the therapist must function in two worlds simultaneously—the worlds of psychotherapy and art—he must be able to integrate different levels of expertise.

Far from being exhaustive in its treatment, this chapter is aimed at helping to point the way for further exploration of the psychodynamic use of materials on the part of all mental health professionals.

Chapter 6

THE INSTITUTION AS A HOLDING ENVIRONMENT FOR THE THERAPIST

Beth Gonzalez Dolginko and Arthur Robbins

As therapists, we are all too well aware that the political climate of an institution has a profound influence on the entire treatment setting. Indeed, we are forced to recognize that a therapist cannot divorce himself from the politics and economics of the institutional structure. Sometimes we become enmeshed in the complex dynamics out of self-preservation, at other times in an attempt to intercede on the part of seemingly helpless patients. A myriad of issues bombards the therapist: What rights does a student intern have? What rights do psychiatric patients have? Does one ever get used to electroconvulsive shock as a treatment modality? What if a patient is being overmedicated or an aide is seen stealing drugs or cigarettes from a patient? When we ourselves come to feel helpless to effect change, how willing or able are we to maintain a holding environment for our patients?

As much as we might wish it otherwise, at times we become no more than mirror reflections of the prevailing administrative climates that filter down from the top. Within that context, the institution can be nurturing, warm, and supportive or engulfing, stultifying, and annihilating. Carrying that parallel further, we may experience our gifts and talents as being accepted and rewarded or feel at the mercy of sadomasochistic play on the part of an administrator. Furthermore, we can experience intense guilt and reprisal or a sense of mastery and self-affirmation.

In all of these dimensions, our efforts and our reactions to the prevailing atmosphere of the institution will ultimately affect the subtle interplay of patient and therapist. Because of that possibility therapists have a responsibility to understand those currents and make efforts to gather around themselves a supportive group of peers and colleagues to support their efforts to provide an appropriate holding environment for their patients. At times we also will need such a support system to protect ourselves from the toxic influence of the institutional climate.

Ideally, we strive to become the containers of our patients' impulses: the hate, the love, and the attendant passions. Our missions invariably become more complex as the institutional model creates additional pressures to contain and to process the feelings generated by the political atmosphere. It is therefore not surprising that therapists who work in institutions often find themselves burning out after a period of time. That condition is reflected in a sense of deadness and apathy. When it happens, one loses the sense of excitement in one's work, and one finds oneself going through the motions without really caring. Psychodynamically, one's defenses will not allow one to invest further and become vulnerable. It becomes necessary to protect oneself from overwhelming hurt, pain, and rage. When burnout becomes extreme, the therapist simply stops working.

As therapists we are constantly faced with the challenge of rising above institutional chaos and still having our mirroring needs for acceptance and recognition met. Some antidotes to the dangers of burnout follow.

1. We need to put limits on our work so that we have time with friends and family.

2. We need to process our reactions concerning both patients and the institutions within which we work. Ideally, that should be done both verbally and nonverbally in peer groups and informally with other mental health colleagues.

3. We need periods of time to get completely away from our work to replenish our personal resources.

4. We must examine our own issues regarding separation and be able to leave a situation that becomes so toxic that it makes our effectiveness and potential growth impossible.

Although professional associations can offer nourishment and replenishment, they can, alas, sometimes present the same problems we encounter at our home base. We see splits (the good versus the bad) and demonstrations of arrogance, withdrawal, and projections as solutions to complex professional problems. Those attitudes filter down into training programs, where teachers express one side or the other of such splits, then push students into one or another warring camp. In the last analysis all of us are very human and need to struggle with the inner problems and attitudes that become projected onto the institution or a particular professional association. Likewise, we can strive to maintain our own separateness and autonomy by avoiding surrender to oppressive introjects that occasionally are embodied in the very institutions and associations that are meant to protect and nourish us.

As a means of preparing students for this complex institutional world, a group of them were encouraged to write and draw about various situations connected with their internships. This process demanded getting in touch with their personal development as creative therapists and being aware of the interrelationships between their development and the "parent" institution.

The students were asked to draw and then describe their feelings and experiences in terms of object relations and relate them to the holding environment (institution). They examined such issues as merger with the staff, supervisors, institutions; their particular fears of engulfment or annihilation; and the particular problems that were either projected or introjected into their relationships with their institutions. Following are the general categories with students' reactions to each.

PERSONAL IDENTITY AS A CREATIVE ARTS THERAPIST

The drawings were done at different times throughout the semester so that the students could watch their evolution as they became both more in touch with institutional issues and more aware of their impending graduation.

> I see myself as a baby anticipating the world's arrival through birth. That infant therapist is willing to expose herself in creating new modalities or methods of healing many different people through this work. Through this willingness to expose, one has to expect to experience growing pains.
> Just as the painter must take the necessary steps to create a finished piece, from stretching the prepared canvas to the final stroke of the brush, I, as a creative arts therapist, am still preparing the canvas surface.

These words, which describe Figure 6-1A, reflect the feelings of a young man in the class who was as much a painter as a healer. He describes his early identity as a therapist as one of feeling like "a side show right out of Ringling Brothers' Circus," in that he was fearful of gaps and silences and felt that sessions had to run smoothly or he would be a failure. Through education, supervision, and experience, he learned that he could maintain the holding environment without having to feel like an entertainer or the savior of the world. His second portrayal of his identity as a creative therapist is one that more cohesively connects the artist and the therapist. Although whimsical in design, it is strong and clear. He grew in his abilities to do effective work therapeutically without denying the strength of his sense of humor. He says in response to this (see Figure 6-1B):

> I see myself as a creative arts therapist who likes nothing better than to help people in need. I feel that it is exciting to be able to share my talents as an artist, and to develop understanding in my patients of their needs and problems. . . . I feel an obligation as an art therapist to create a pleasant working situation to enable my patients to develop creative alternatives.

A mature woman in the class who had raised a family, worked in a special education setting, and had done some peer

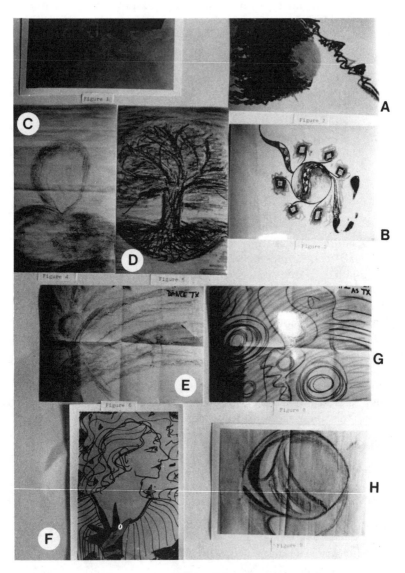

Figure 6-1.

counseling for a number of years, describes herself (Figure 6-1C) as follows:

> . . . organic soft form, its rounded edges flowing into a representation of a torso mother/child image. . . the image is of a unit with the mother holding the infant in her arms and cradling or nursing the infant. I realize that my strength as a therapist is the mothering quality that I bring to a situation.

As the semester progressed, she became more aware of a variety of professional opportunities opening up to her. She then did the drawing in Figure 6-1D and noted:

> . . . a tree located in the center of the paper within a circle. The tree shows a strong root system with a solid trunk and a network of branches. The leaves are lighter and the colors seem to indicate spring—the beginning of new life. It is expansive and provides openness in order to allow the light to shine through. Elements of fantasy are indicated by the use of purple and yellow in the tree itself. I feel this drawing indicates a strong self-identity, and with the help of the root system and the elements of nourishment, this tree will be around a long time. And it will undergo many changes!

An interesting view is offered by a dance therapy student in the class who was also employed as a dance therapist. Her first "identity as a creative arts therapist" shows what she describes as an almost primitive idealization of the supervisor, the large figure included in her self-identity (Figure 6-1E). The class then came in touch with the need for the intern or young professional to have role models to idealize. These same role models may later be rejected or "fall from grace" as the "new" creative therapist struggles for his own identity and style.

In Figure 6-1F, there is more of a feeling of differentiation, and the light and airy quality seen in Figure 6-1E is not quite so prominent. There is a more realistic sense of boundaries, with a fair mix of nurturing strength and watchful anxiety, as seen in the Picasso eye on the therapist figure. The ability to hold the patient figure amid interference is obvious.

Finally, it is interesting to look at drawings done by two students in very different relationships to the graduate program. One student held an unusual position in the group in that she was new to the program. She described her identity, as seen in Figure 6-1G, this way:

> I am still green and open. I fill the page with my hopes
> and expectations; my wide-eyed wonder, and innocence. I
> am in profile, as I am aware on some level that this is not
> a fully rounded representation.

Compare her words to those of the student very near the end of her training who, because of personal obligations, has had to spend more than the usual 2 years of full-time work to complete her degree (Figure 6-1H).

> I am . . . a cosmic egg . . . that has been "cracked" and
> has opened, which, I feel, is indicative of my own identity.
> I don't feel the initial anxiety about "who" this art therapist
> is, but see it as a flexible role that is constantly in a state of
> flux and growth. I also don't feel so dependent upon the
> institution as part of my professional identity, but see it as
> but one facet.

It would be interesting to see this student draw a picture 5 years down the road of institutional practice to see how she comes to deal with the machinations and politics of that setting.

THE INTERN IN THE INSTITUTION

As can be expected, this topic raised a great deal of feeling and discussion. By and large, the institution was seen as the restricting and almighty parent with the medical staff standing at the right hand of this powerful Zeus. Working under the auspices of an activity or recreation department, students often felt out of place and/or misunderstood. To add insult to injury, the work done with patients was often devalued, patronized, or undermined.

Students were encouraged to examine their artwork along

with their feelings to become aware of transferential issues with the institution or a supervisor. By taking the responsibility in this way, students were able to shed some of their helplessness and to courageously take steps to ameliorate difficult situations.

One woman was able to experience what patients must feel on admission to a short-term hospital situation as she thought about her training experience.

> Just as the decompensated patient is admitted and cared for until recompensation, my own experience was similar. I was cared for of a short duration and then quickly, I was on my own.

The same student described the restrictions placed on her interventions by the hospital. Because the hospital was run by the Catholic Church, she was instructed that it was "improper" to counsel patients regarding birth control, abortions, divorce, or any other topics thought taboo by the church. She discusses Figure 6-2A this way:

> ... I have not completely identified my role with the hospital. The hospital in my drawing is hardly discernible except for the large cross at the top. I (the circle) am placed in the art room, yet also outside the hospital. There is marked ambivalence in the drawing signifying my own ambivalence. The entire drawing appears laden with anxiety.

Several of the students ran up against narcissictic institutions and narcissistic directors. This was often the result of participation in a newly formed program. If the programs were also headed by those who had designed them, double jeopardy was in order. Such programs or institutions were often dogmatic or had a point to make, and students would be "punished" if they failed to reflect the narcissistic parent.

One student, who had developed her own innovative program housed within a very dogmatic agency, had these feelings (Figure 6-2B):

> One of the reasons for conflicts over ideologies that arose ... was the need on the part of the director for a

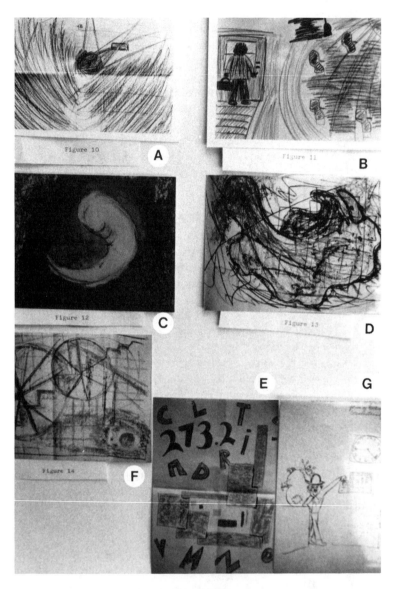

Figure 6-2.

perfect mirror. . . . In keeping with the narcissistic character, I believe the director had idealized me, catering to my every need, only to be disappointed later on.

Here I stand with my hand on the doorknob looking in and considering whether or not to enter. Empty chairs on the right illustrate my constant plight to attract people to my groups, with the dark, foreboding figure overhead representing the director. . . . I was bringing totally new ideas which rocked the boat.

Another student became quite lost within the narcissictic institution because of her inability to identify and separate her own narcissistic issues. Her "identity as a creative arts therapist" drawing became merged with her drawing of her "self in the institution" when it came to processing (Figure 6-2C).

I am the embryo held in my own calm blue holding environment. I am not yet fully formed, and I hide inside while the world outside is hot and dark and threatening. I was reluctant to meet the demands that are now being made of me. I was a "good" girl. I did my work and I didn't want anyone to interfere. . . . I became stubborn and rejected the parent (institution) which had ignored me for so long. I was shocked and angry at the demands and refused to go out in the chaos.

She later stood back from much of the chaos and began to see the institution as polarizing into two groups, the super-doers and the isolators:

The super-doers became run down and very resentful because of all their extra duties. They felt taken advantage of and this resentment showed itself in all kinds of acting-out behavior.

She goes on to discuss her drawing of herself in the institution in this manner (Figure 6-2D):

I'm all goodness over which the institution slashes back and forth interrupting and pinning down my creativity. I

am confused and losing a grip on my wholeness. My shape
is no longer contained. I am becoming unsure of myself
because the "parent" has changed and I am unsure of it.

It is understandable how such a difficult situation could cause a
therapist to become ineffective in his work with patients. The
chaos and confusion this therapist felt is obvious in her drawing.

Being a creative therapist in a very structured and rigid setting, such as a teaching hospital, has advantages and disadvan-
tages. Although the setting is stimulating and can be innovative,
the medical model can be stultifying if one is attempting to establish an identity other than one based on that model or have
his input heard. One man in the class gave an introspective account of his own separation–individuation process from such an
institution. He was able to look at both the good and bad in his
experiences and feel his own burnout as a process through which
to examine who he was and where he was, or was not, going.
His drawing of himself in the institution shows many letters and
numbers, as these are a part of the everyday life of diagnosis,
medication, and the like in a big hospital. He describes Figure
6-2E this way:

> The emphasis on the borders, and the care taken to
> define each space can suggest the importance of the merger–
> differentiation issues for the artist . . . the black/gray dom-
> inance . . . suggests a lack of affect, an impersonality. [The
> letters and the numbers] are images to mirror a stifling in-
> stitutional atmosphere filled with a rational, verbal, left-
> hemisphere orientation.

Another student struggled with many of the same feelings
and issues in her work in a teaching hospital.

> The institution asks for conformity, rigidity, and total
> monotheistic devotion. One must give up one's identity if
> one is incorporated into the institution. On the other hand,
> rebellion means that one turns away from the support, sur-
> vival, and structure provided by the parent institution. . . .
> We must be aware of the cultural dualism drawn between

techne and psyche and how this may cause us to perpetuate our seeing the institution as all bad because of its tyranny over us. Thus, we split our own natures. Also, if our object representation is split, so is our self-representation, as the two are co-created. We must then be at least two people in our workplace.

The struggle between the artist and the therapist in all of us can be gratified or frustrated depending on the institution. Which department houses the creative arts therapist and how the institution sees the art therapist's role are but two of the components of this picture. One woman employed in a large state facility shared these feelings after doing Figure 6-2F:

> To become my own person as an art therapist is primarily a battle that rages within me. I am afraid to "hatch" out of that purple egglike encasement, and when I try it, it is anxiety-producing. In one way, it is effortless to be assimilated into the recreation aspect of my job. I say very little of who I am and no one sees me as different from the other rehabilitation staff, or so it appears to me. But there are so many times when it bothers me. I am not an arts and crafts person, yet much of what I do is just that . . . I hate playing bingo! At times it is not too difficult to give in to the part of me that says, "I am a recreation person. What difference does it make anyway? The pay and the benefits are all the same."

Finally, one man whimsically processed the plight of the bohemian part of the artist within as contrasted with the rigid and unbending authority of the institution. He was able to explore his own acting-out behavior and see it as induced by the institution, while simultaneously accepting his responsibility in the given situation. He discussed Figure 6-2G this way:

> My resisting formal structure took place in tardiness. . . .
> I felt ripped off as an intern: overworked and dumped on.

I conducted nine workshops in 4 days (more than anyone else in this department working 5 days) and carried two individuals as a caseload. Three different times my notes about patients' progress went into treatment plans with somebody else's name on it. . . . I found myself always acting out as a scapegoat in order to preserve my artistic identity as a freelance, maverick type. Meanwhile, though, my art was suffering greatly.

Despite negative transferences toward the institution, the students were able to understand the importance of working within a system and having their work recognized and respected. They were able to realize that they needed to adapt and seek support within the setting, even when it meant coming to terms with difficult administrative issues.

A further word is in order here regarding the struggle between the administrative pressures of an agency, whose mission is to serve the community, and the individual needs of the patients. This conflict places the therapist in a constant bind. The spirit of an artist is one that is associated with changing boundaries, redefining self, and moving into alternate states of consciousness. Institutions tend to move toward homeostasis and stabilization. Administrators can mediate those opposing forces or surrender the agency to one force or another. More often than not, we find the wish for individuality and originality supressed when it conflicts with the agency mission. In the process there are many narcissistic wounds encountered and inflicted that require soothing and processing.

I have the hope that some of us will be idealistic, courageous, and persevering enough to form our own institutions to serve the needs of our patients better as well as to provide an environment where art therapists can work more effectively. This latter alternative requires a good deal of energy and idealism but would be well worth the attempt for those with the patience and fortitude. In the process, however, we would do well to remember that even the stoutest of idealists will come up against some of the very problems they encountered and battled in more traditional settings.

THE TREATMENT TEAM AND SUPERVISORS

One student's reflections concerning the coming together of a treatment team were these:

> Both the rational and the intuitive have a place in any system. It is true we, in our current Western culture, have little tolerance for paradox . . . it is only through our contact with the Eastern mind that we have learned that all apparent opposites contain the seeds of one another. To freeze either side in negativity is to tear asunder aspects that must find rapport with one another to touch the dynamic from which creativity springs.

Her drawing of the treatment team indicates an attempt, which she sees as an important one, to represent how the rational and intuitive can come together to do effective and creative treatment. Of Figure 6-3A, she says:

> The art therapist is the only one who exists in a way that is ambiguous and moving. We may feel unsure and insecure, but our ambiguity allows us to give care on many different levels. Perhaps this may link other forms of care our patients receive. We are, however, isolated in this position and must reach out and introduce ourselves.

Another student felt this isolation from the treatment team more acutely, as she was subjected to disruptive changes within the team. The original supervisor with whom she was supposed to work left for another job. The second supervisor, with whom she felt connected and from whom she felt support, was let go because she did not fit with the treatment team. That situation would be understandably upsetting. In Figure 6-3B she draws herself very much apart from the treatment team:

> Yep, that's me sprawled out on the chairs, sitting in the playroom. The playroom is a safe place. I'm trying to be what I want to be in there, but I don't look very happy. I

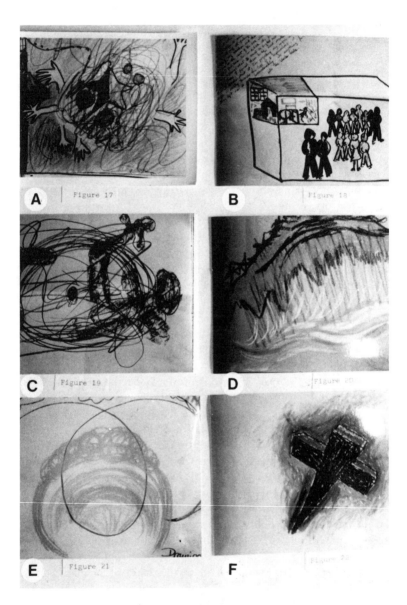

Figure 6-3.

look limp and running out of life. The round black table is
ominous, isn't it? It's where I can dump all my ill feelings,
sorrow, anger, bad feelings about myself, my situation, and
the staff. The staff takes up all the room in the rest of the
box I'm in. I've been making lots of boxes. I feel like I'm
in a box. The people consist of the kids and the staff—
strange that two should be singled out so strongly in black.
While I drew them, I figured them to be head people, like
psychiatrists. But now that I think about it, I'm projecting
my anger onto head staff people. The anger is really toward
the loss of two supervisors. I feel stranded and alone. They
left me so inconsiderately. Is anything fair? I'm trying not
to sink into the black table.

She continues to use the black in Figure 6-3C, which represents
her supervisor. The black represents the loss. The amorphous
shape seems symbolic of her being on her own, yet the forms
are flowing and flexible and may indicate an ability on her part
to fit into the treatment team even though she was "abandoned"
by the supervisor who could not.

Many of the students had positive transferences to their supervisors. Others, however, had difficulty connecting for one
reason or another. Through the drawing of the treatment team
and then of their supervisors, the students were able to see how
they represented their supervisors as members of the larger
groups and then as individuals. Often, as previously mentioned,
students' own identities were based on their perceptions of and
relatedness to their supervisors. Through the exercise students
could separate and individuate from their supervisors and could
explore who they were as growing professionals.

One student felt misunderstood by a supervisor who seemed
to project a great deal of inadequacy onto her. The situation was
an unusual one in which the supervisor had a great deal of art
education experience but no real art therapy training. She herself
was considering furthering her education in the field of art therapy. In the meantime that made for ill feelings on both sides
because neither was able to emerge as supervisor. Of Figure 6-
3D the student says:

> I am the more solid form underneath. I am supporting
> myself as well as showing growth. My supervisor is the similar
> but more erratic form above me. She is not formed because
> she is not sure of what she is. She was forced to look at
> herself and her capabilities, and I only validated her ina-
> bilities.

As in the ending of all relationships, there are a number of feelings concerning what is good, what is bad, what we have learned, and what we will miss in one another. One student who had been working with a private supervisor for 2 years, had had a very good experience. She learned a great deal about all the expressive therapies. As she approached termination, she became aware of her supervisor devaluing her more, while tightening her fists and body posture whenever challenged by the student. This insightful student began to see that her supervisor was be-having like an angry or envious parent might toward a successful child. She felt saddened by that, as it colored their termination in a way she had not anticipated. After doing Figure 6-3E she realized that the image was highly defensive, and she got in touch with what was going on in the relationship. She was able to main-tain distance and accept the good and bad, as she described the colors as intense yet balanced.

Involved in a supervisory relationship are all the feelings associated with such important themes as feeding, control, sup-port, and separation. Ideally, the mission of the supervisory re-lationship is one of aiding and facilitating the autonomous de-velopment of the student. At the same time, however, supervisors must reflect the needs and aspirations of the agency they serve. As a result, they are placed in dual roles of serving the needs of their supervisees while having to remain within bounds of the agencies' missions. Ideally, there should not be a conflict in this area. However, often the supervisor is placed in the most difficult position of feeling identified with a particular student whose style is divergent from those of a particular agency. For a supervisor, the maintenance of one's autonomy can be as dif-ficult as it is for a student. The job demands a high degree of emotional maturity.

COUNTERTRANSFERENCE

One of the most important jobs of the supervisory situation is to enable students to become aware of their countertransference reactions to patients and to manage those feelings. Drawing in response to those feelings has been an effective tool when working with therapists. Within large institutions, though, the student is exposed to many issues that interfere with the treatment and affect the countertransference in regard to race, religion, sex, age, and ethnicity. In this exercise the students were instructed to draw a patient with whom they were feeling intense intergroup issues. Many students were able to share their prejudices and fears in a way that could productively help them to intervene with particular patients with whom they felt stuck.

One man described his feelings with a difficult patient in this way after doing Figure 6-3F:

> With its various degrees of hue, the engulfing cross burned like an iron-hot spike which was bound for my heart: the final blow as a caring therapist. This iron-hot spike of a cross is G. She is a forty-four-year-old schizophrenic Orthodox Jewish woman. Resembling Mel Blanc's looney-tune character, the Tasmanian Devil, but heavier and wearing glasses, she spins around you kicking up verbiage, all in the attempt to explain the vast chaos of the world in which she lives. . . . I was caught up in a countertransference of a stereotype—a loud Jewish woman that one would only view on a show such as Saturday Night Live!

Her reactions reinforced his feelings as she accused him of antisemitism when he scheduled a Friday afternoon group. Any attempts on his part to show some concern caused her to recoil, as she transferred her feelings onto him of an uncaring son, similar in age to the therapist. The student was able to bring his feelings of anger and resentment to the treatment team and to his supervisor. By doing so he was able to see that she induced such feelings in many others. He was then able to separate the cultural issues and deal with them. The treatment then could continue in a less contaminated and more productive direction.

The exploration of countertransference issues within the supervisory relationship can provoke a great deal of anxiety on the part of the supervisee. Obviously, a good deal of security must be built into the relationship for a supervisee to explore his feelings regarding patients, especially when an environment is toxic or stressful.

Supervision can be reduced to an intrusive interrogation which, at best, provides spurious material; however, even in the most secure of circumstances the supervisor and supervisee must be very clear as to their boundaries between supervision and therapy. Two useful criteria can be employed: does the material under discussion interfere with the flow of the therapeutic process, and does it interfere with the supervisee becoming a more effective therapist? These criteria provide a good deal of latitude and require considerable judgment on the part of the supervisor. The supervisor cannot work out or solve problems through supervision but can at least identify issues. Even in these instances, once a negative transference is directed toward the supervisor, the supervisory relationship is no longer a positive holding environment within which learning can take place.

The ability to work with personal material within the supervisory relationship implies that the student is already well into his own treatment and has sufficient resources and boundaries to be able to move back and forth from a personal exploration to the particular therapeutic area being investigated. For many supervisees that difficult back-and-forth oscillation is too difficult and creates confusion and loss of boundaries. When that occurs, it is best for the supervisor to maintain a very clear structure and to avoid too deep an exploration of countertransference material. The supervisee in such instances is not ready to integrate this kind of material.

CONCLUSION

As therapists we must be aware that we do not work in a vacuum. For that reason, it is important to look at those issues and situations that will have an effect on the treatment process. Denying that those issues exist is like denying that we are all artists first. As artists we can learn to ebb and flow in an ongoing evolutionary process, so that we leave a little piece of us behind while we take a valuable lesson ahead.

Figures 6-4A and 6-4B were two drawings done by a student at the beginning and at the end of the series: that is, both are "your identity as a creative arts therapist" drawings. Figure 6-4A looks like a chambered nautilus with tearlike sunshine emanating from it. The woman who drew it is hearing impaired. Perhaps part of what helped her to become a therapist was a sense of empathy stemming from living with hearing loss. Figure 6-4B is a peaceful beach scene. Although the student is longing for this relaxation after such intense training, it seems that the open and expansive quality may represent her as yet unformed but hopeful future. The horizon is not quite clear as she begins her professional journey. Still, her feeling is that the sky is the limit.

Comparing those two pictures, we see that there is a difference in the use of internal versus external space. Although both are lovely, the second and later drawing is considerably more global in its scope and may represent the woman's journey from

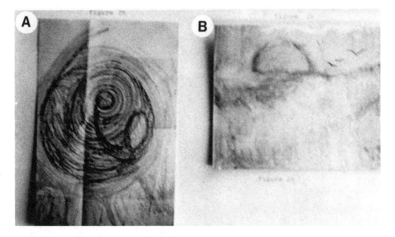

Figure 6-4.

a more introverted place to one of greater awareness and experience. That was generally experienced by the whole class.

Our effectiveness as therapists working within agencies and institutions is absolutely dependent on our ability to tap the creative process, look within ourselves, and respond to patients' and environmental currents in creative ways. Utilizing visual representations of issues encountered in our work places can be invaluable in that process.

Chapter 7

THE USE OF VISUAL PERCEPTION AS AN AIDE IN PLANNING SHORT-TERM TREATMENT GOALS

The multiple, complex problems facing the fledgling therapist in a short-term institutional setting can easily promote professional burnout if a means is not found to organize the conflicting issues and formulate directions and goals. The nature of such problems fall into the broad categories of unclear job descriptions and institutional expectations, clinical issues, and the personal resources and limitations of individual therapists.

The sheer number of patients of diverse diagnoses and needs becomes a challenge in and of itself. Diagnostic categories range from thought disorders and affect mood states to organic syndromes and an occasional so-called normal on the mend after a breakdown. Often, the number of patients in each session fluctuates, with up to 15 or 20 members moving in and out of the group in any one session. What's more, this already frustrating situation exists within a treatment system that advocates short-term intervention. Add to that the therapist's own countertransference reactions, cognitive despair, and an intense need to survive, and it's hardly wonder that the therapist begins to question the possibility of anything being accomplished. Burnout is all too common.

In general, treatment is ego-oriented to reinforce such ego skills as judgment, the use of verbalization, reality testing, and an integration of image, thought, body consciousness, and action. Rules and limits are set to create a safe holding environment for the group. Treatment plans and choices of activities serve multiple goals. They serve to govern the stimulation level of the group as a whole but also address the relative degrees of fear of intrusion and need for touch and contact of individuals. The selection of materials and theme also are structured to help clarify the relationship of the patient to his group, hospital, and perhaps to the community to which he will return. Above all, the therapist must be flexible enough to modify plans depending on the energy level and immediate issues of the group members in any given session.

In this whirlpool of conflicting demands and needs it is easy for the therapist to feel as though no room exists for his own creative energy. Paradoxically, it is from those personal creative juices that insight and direction can emerge.

The method for harnessing that creative force is fairly simple. After the therapist's first session with a new group he draws a free-form impression of the group. The analysis of that drawing can be made along such aesthetic lines as form, shape, balance, the use of color, and integration of the theme, all of which have parallel psychodynamic implications. As in working with dreams, the therapist's unconscious perception of his therapeutic experience is employed to organize the subliminal impressions not readily accessible pertaining to a particular group experience. That perception will invariably be affected by and intermixed with the therapist's countertransference reactions. Thus, the drawing that emerges makes a statement about the complex interconnections of the therapist and the group with all the inherent limitations and forces at work.

Ideally, several such impressions of a group would be drawn over time. Each drawing would pose a problem to challenge the artist in the therapist. With each attempt, perceptions would be organized and reorganized, the therapist would struggle with differentiation and integration in the drawing, and finally, a resolution of sorts would emerge in the completed artwork. That creative process could then be used to give direction to treatment planning as the parallels between the aesthetic issues and the psychodynamic issues of the group were examined.

Imperative in such a technique is the avoidance of the individual issues of each patient. The goal is an overall gestalt perception of the group process at work. For example, the therapist's use of color and form might make his drawing look chaotic. The drawing might lack a central theme, be fragmented, or lack organization in choice of color. The therapist/artist would attempt to rework the drawing aesthetically to give it more balance and integration. Remember that each drawing is looked at not only along aesthetic lines, but also in terms of what recommendations can be elicited pertaining to dynamics in and potential directions for the group. Inherent in such revisions are the emotional limitations of the therapist and the dynamics of group process.

Following are some examples of the procedure used by beginning therapy students. Each drew his impressions of an initial group experience in a short-term treatment facility, then brought the drawing to class for analysis.

The first picture belongs to an intern assigned to a children's hospital dayroom where the patients are in the process of recovering from a variety of physical illnesses (Figure 7-1A). Some children are hospitalized for a very short time; others stay for a protracted period. As the student draws her first picture, she is immediately aware of the gray center. She decides that represents the hub of activity and the place where conflicts and fantasies are worked through using a variety of nonverbal media. She also hypothesizes that it represents the center of her own uncertainty and confusion as to what is really going on.

As she observes the picture, she is struck by the frameless quality of the bright colors reaching out of the picture. As she reviews her picture, it is clear that she has captured the life, color, action, and energy that symbolizes the busyness and activity of the dayroom. She is also aware, however, that the individual components seem to lack an overall cohesiveness. As that perception dawns, the student realizes that it will take her time to sharpen her impressions so the picture can have a more integrated quality. She recognizes that her typical reaction to stress is to move toward fragmentation, and now she needs to put the separate parts together.

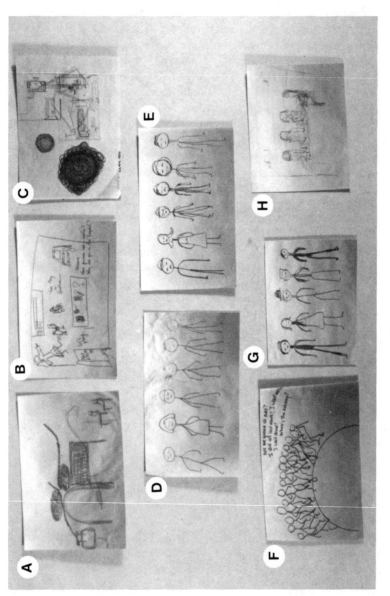

Figure 7-1.

On further reflection, she associates the lack of a frame with her relationship to the hospital structure. She rarely uses medical records or consults with medical personnel. She feels isolated, alone, and very confused. Just as the gray table stands out, needing some kind of connection with the forces surrounding it, so the therapist too needs connection with the greater hospital system surrounding her patients. She becomes aware of her need for consultation and for review of the records of each child to facilitate more appropriate treatment planning. It will take time, but by utilizing the hospital's structure to get more information she will have a better sense of the individual children and, in turn, a more defined sense of the group.

The second drawing represents the work of a student placed in the same institution (Figure 7-1B). It is apparent here how strongly the personal limitations and character of each student determines the specific actions and style of treatment implementation. This picture is composed of tight little places and fragments with little connection to one another. There seems to be a lack of focus or direction to the picture. In contrast to the first picture, where the student depicts the ambience of the room, albeit compartmentalized, this student focuses on the individual components, like balls of energy that require structure, direction, and thrust. She stands cramped in the corner looking helpless. As she further talks about the picture, she realizes that the words that she gives each component do not really help make connections. Her compartmentalization mirrors her defenses as she attempts to order the distress of an overwhelming situation.

She draws a second picture, and there she sketches a blueprint of the room, a schematic impression of the activity and the various forces at work (Figure 7-1C). The second drawing serves the adaptive purpose of giving her some emotional distance, firming up her defenses, and lending some degree of control and organization to her experience.

She then proceeds to draw a mandala in the hope of centering her feelings and finding a sense of wholeness. The mandala is surrounded by a whirling black mass, which symbolically protects her inner core of warmth and expressiveness. Finally, in the third mandala, the student approaches some sense of wholeness. That carries over to the therapeutic situation where she realizes she must attempt to center herself in the playroom if she is to be able to respond directly and empathetically to her patients.

In both examples the treatment planning is directly tied to the attitudinal set of the therapist rather than to the organization of a particular activity. The awareness of those inner perceptions becomes the fulcrum for changes in the therapeutic approach to a group's activities.

The next example represents several sessions of work by a student assigned to the dayroom of an outpatient alcohol clinic (Figure 7-1D). As she looks at her drawings, she sees the extreme isolation and passivity of her patients in the first drawing. She observes how alone and disconnected from one another they appear. She sees separate islands of emptiness, all crying out for individuation but with cries ever so far away and cut off from awareness.

With that perception, the student designs an exercise to elicit change. She asks the group first to draw a house, then to take one part of that house and magnify it. Finally, the therapist encourages her patients to put people inside their individual houses. The exercise is meant to afford each patient a glimpse at his inner world and to promote awareness of and connection with one another and significant others.

After that exercise the student brings a second picture of her group to class (Figure 7-1E). The members of the group appear clearer and more recognizable than in the first picture but still passive and withdrawn. She recognizes that she now has a better sense of her patients as discrete individuals but that she needs to design further exercises to facilitate their being more in touch with themselves and others.

The next picture represents the work of a student placed in a clinic, also with alcoholics, on an outpatient basis (Figure 7-1F). As she draws her work, the student comments that she is very much aware of the lack of distinctiveness and individuality of the group members. They seem to huddle together to form a faceless crowd. She experiences their helplessness and also is aware of their hungry need for support. The student is surprised by the lack of individuality with which she depicts her patients, for she had thought she had a better sense of their separateness.

On the basis of that picture the student decides to ask the group to compose masks. Her rationale for that exercise is that the masks give patients an opportunity for protection while providing expressions of individuality. She reports that there is much excitement and involvement with the exercise.

Her second picture is the result of her experience with the exercise of the masks (Figure 7-1G). The individual participants of her group are now more clearly defined and are not so huddled together in an undefined mass. She also reports that she feels more related to and connected with her group.

The next picture represents the impressions of a student placed in a nursery school (Figure 7-1H). She becomes immediately aware of the somberness of her colors and the stiffness and rigidity of the participants in her group. They all look so contained, terribly restricted in their spontaneity. On the basis of that picture, the student intends to introduce more unstructured art materials and colors to encourage greater expression and looser interaction between group members.

The last example represents the work of a student who is placed in a psychiatric day-care center. He was aware of the busyness of his first picture and attempted to organize it and give his drawing more cohesiveness (picture not shown). After some reflection, however, he recognized that his original picture possessed more energy and originality and realized that his need for order could rob the energy of its authenticity. It is important to remember that with this technique, the student attempts to improve the work aesthetically, and only after the second picture is drawn can psychological implications be made. Otherwise, the preconscious organization becomes contaminated with intellectualizations.

In summary, therapist's drawings of initial group experiences can serve as a means to order conscious and subliminal perceptions. Such externalization and structuring of chaotic material gives the therapist an opportunity for differentiation and organization, as well as for personal centering. In turn, further understanding and cohesion allow the therapist to plan appropriate treatment interventions that take into account his emotional resources and limitations, as well as the particular dynamics of any given group. All too often therapists forget to tap their innate strengths and creativity. It is hoped that the procedure described above illustrates how the artistry and creativity of the artist in the therapist can offer something unique in treatment planning.

Part II

CLINICAL APPLICATIONS

Chapter 8

TRANSFERENCE AND COUNTERTRANSFERENCE WITHIN THE SCHIZOID PHENOMENON*

Several factors determine the direction and nuances of any given creative arts therapy treatment. They include the problems presented by the patient, the particular personality and character of the therapist, and frequently the institutional goals and limitations that stem from a team approach. Coloring all three factors, however, are issues of transference and countertransference.

I refer the reader to a previously published work (LaMonica & Robbins, 1980) for a lengthy discussion of the historical and technical changes in conceptualization of those two phenomena. Here I would like briefly to talk about the broader, "totalistic" meanings and implications these terms have taken on since Freud originally defined them. The totalistic concept defines transference as those emotions, attitudes, or perceptions from the past that the patient brings to the relationship, countertransference as the total emotional response of the therapist to the patient.

*Presented as part of a panel at the Twelfth Annual Conference of the American Art Therapy Association, Liberty, New York, October 22–25, 1981. The theoretical section pertinent to transference. Previously published in the *American Journal of Art Therapy*, Oct. 1981.

Where Freud and classical psychoanalysts have seen counter-transference as a distortion that impedes therapy, followers of the totalistic concept, frequently clinicians who work with more disturbed patients, see countertransference as a tool with which to understand patients' dynamics better. The broader definition maintains that the countertransference phenomenon reflects not only the realistic and neurotic issues of the therapist but also reactions to the patient's reality and transference that help the therapist better to understand the patient's unconscious behavior, particularly as associated with early object relations. Such concepts as empathy, transient trial identification, and intuition are included here.

Winnicott's (1971) "primary creativity," mentioned in Chapter 2, helps to explain the intertwining of transference/counter-transference, developmental issues, and creativity in the therapeutic process. In Winnicott's schema, the core of self-esteem and the most basic dedifferentiation between inside and outside, self and other, come from the time when the mother uses her intuitive, coenesthetic self to communicate and receive communications on a visceral, sensorimotor level. The looking, cooing, singing, rocking, playing, physical caring create a fabric—a space, if you will—where the chaotic stimuli are organized and fed back to the infant by the "good enough" mother in a way that gives cohesiveness to the newborn's experiences. Over time that space evolves to promote growth and discovery of the child's unique sense of self and recognition of the similarities and differences between that self and significant others in the baby's environment.

If the "good enough" mother is pictured as a container for the confusing and at times overwhelming stimuli from the infant's surroundings, one can imagine a pathological relationship as one in which that metaphorical container breaks, spills over, leaks, or is essentially absent. With inadequate help in organizing stimuli from the environment, what the infant takes in will be poorly assimilated and will often break through the child's stimulus barrier to overwhelm his fragile sense of existence. Because no infant can exist in complete isolation, the child with inadequate mothering will create his own organizer for primary experiences.

However, that substitute mother inevitably reflects its creator's experience; therefore, frightening creatures emerge in the child's representational world—such as witches with piercing eyes and incomplete breasts. All of that interferes with the development of a real self. Reality provokes fear and anxiety and is splintered by fragmented perceptions. Protection against fragmentation is supplied by the creation of a grandiose self that becomes a safe stronghold. People may be perceived as divided into totally good and totally bad. Massive defenses develop that further distort reality. Here we see the beginnings of excessive projection, introjection, and denial.

Therapy, then, becomes a means to refight the lost battles and to complete unfinished dialogues. If nothing else, it is a process through which one revisits relationships that have been associated with loss, annihilation, pain, and love, and in which the polarities and paradoxes inherent in relationships are reworked so that the painful process of leave-taking can proceed. A creative arts therapist must create an environment where this series of separations and the consequent renewal and regeneration of self can take place.

Sometimes the patient needs only the quiet, empathic presence of the therapist to facilitate the process of giving symbolic form to the complex, nonverbal affects, witches, fantasies, and images that characterize primary process thinking and codify early experiences. For such a patient a more active intervention on the part of the therapist would be too intrusive. That is particularly relevant for severe borderline and psychotic conditions where the overt transference becomes too charged to work through in the real relationship. Consequently, an art form maintains integrity and becomes the organizer of the therapeutic process.

In other instances, however, patients require that the therapist do something about the psychic material that is externalized in the art work. They request, covertly or overtly, help in the process of reorganization. The therapist becomes the new parent who apprehends the impressions and affects of the patient's lost past, reorganizes them, and feeds them back in a more assimilable form. As the therapist helps the patient to mend internal splits, to reconcile the polarities of raging hate and love, and to heal the pain of loss and separation, he promotes what is technically called neutralization.

Art alone is not the main force that makes leave-taking possible. In addition to art media, the art therapist uses empathy, recognition, and constancy to make up for the preverbal deficiencies of mothering that (because they are preverbal) cannot easily be reduced to words.

Art becomes the bridge for deep communications. What the therapist does with those communications will depend not only on the patient's needs and the institution's structure but also on the therapist's emotional receptivity and ability to call on personal images and symbols with which to help the patient explore and develop his own images. The therapist moves back and forth between primary and secondary processes, between a relationship mediated by deep nonverbal symbols and the work of organizing those experiences so they can be reflected back to the patient with greater coherence and meaning. A playful attitude on the part of the therapist makes it easier to move in and out of those positions and to work both reparatively and transferentially. Art and creativity, then, can be useful in several ways: they may help initiate contact, establish rapport, serve as a means to externalize and concretize inner images and affects from the past, clarify transference/countertransference manifestations, and provide a safe frame within which to organize patients' communications.

Each therapy session becomes a symbolic dialogue in which both patient and therapist struggle with their respective ghosts and demons. It is hoped that the therapist will be more in charge of the process than the patients, but the therapist should not fool himself with false notions of professionalism or objectivity. By the very nature of their profession art therapists, more than other members of the therapeutic team, are especially vulnerable to the primitive, nonverbal messages that constitute so large a portion of communication on the part of psychotic and borderline patients and those suffering from character disorders. In struggling to avoid the subtle, primitive invasions of their egos, art therapists will from time to time employ their own particular defenses, such as overidealization, distancing, defensive anger, and so on. Countertransference reactions are often unavoidable as art therapists move with their patients into deep, uncharted, nonverbal territory, where their own past fears are invariably touched on regardless of how much personal treatment they have undergone. Under such circumstances art and creativity can be used to mask countertransference reactions and to keep the therapist at a comfortable distance from the very patients he is trying to reach.

Thus, each therapist brings to treatment his own particular style, expectations, and attitudes from the past that will have an important impact on the patient's communications. Paradoxically, therapists' effectiveness will be determined partly by their ability to untangle themselves from countertransference reactions so that they can listen and respond effectively to the patient. Both therapist and patient are in treatment within any given art therapy relationship, each struggling with his particular attachments to the past and emotional responses to the other.

Three vignettes follow of patients who are currently in long-term treatment with the author. Although superficially appearing different in terms of mood, defenses, and adaptive structures, all three present a schizoid core of loneliness and desperation. Jan appears superficially charming, erotic, almost hysterical, whereas Rebecca presents abject terror, seeing danger everywhere, reminiscent of a cornered cat ready to strike out at anything that moves. She comes close to paranoia in her distrust of the world. Bob, our third case, is riddled with body tensions, anger, sadness, depression, all held very tightly. What all three hold in common are deeply covered islands of loneliness and alienation.

Because the covers and moods of Jan, Rebecca, and Bob are so different, so too are the holding environments. The transference/countertransference phenomena reflect the paradox of wanting to be close and held while pushing away. The patients have differing fears of control, possession, and overwhelming demands, but really each is saying in his or her own way that the price of contact and closeness is too great, all the while searching for and craving those very things.

For true reorganization of the personality to take place, these patients, as well as the therapist, must touch these rock-bottom parts of their personalities. Treatment holds the hope that feelings of loneliness and isolation can be touched, that closeness can be had.

JAN[1]

When Jan first entered my office I was immediately aware of her eyes with their sad, liquid emptiness. Her face was expressionless, with an occasional smile breaking through. At forty-seven she was unmarried and very tired. As her story unfolded, I learned that she did not need to work, for she had a small income from her parents' estate. That should have allowed her some ease, but she busily, even frantically, moved from one task to another. She felt her life rush by her, becoming increasingly aware that the span of one's life was not endless. Paradoxically, she also felt younger than her age.

Life had been a series of short and long love affairs for this woman. Some dissolved before they began; others were filled with pain and remorse. As she talked in a vague poetic way, I was interested and intrigued but strangely disconnected. There was an ethereal quality about this patient that defied solidity or definition. The one thing that came through loud and strong was the depth of her loneliness and sense of being lost. I felt the impulse to be warm and protective even as she eluded me, like sand slipping through my fingers. I was reminded of an old movie, *Hiroshima Mon Amour,* the story of a young woman's personal disaster as mirrored in an atomic holocaust. Eroticism offered a desperate anchor in the midst of a chaotic world.

I asked Jan to draw a picture about herself, with the hope that I would get a more defined picture of the inner world in which she dwelt. She protested: "I don't have enough time to do it in the session." I asked if she would be willing to draw something about herself at home. She readily agreed.

Next session she brought me a set of pictures, all looking quickly drawn in a monochromatic blue. There was movement in her drawings, but a lack of dimension. Although Jan was particularly pleased with one picture that she said described the sen-

[1]Some of this material will appear in Rubin, J. Approaches To Art Therapy; Brunner/Mazer, N.Y. In press.

sual part of herself, the part that craves contact and needs to be touched, she had nothing else to say about that drawing (Figure 8-1A). She did give some information about the other pictures, however. The hands reaching out represented the part of herself that needed to be a part of something bigger (Figures 8-1B, 8-1C). In the fourth picture, which represented the Jewish community she loved, she expanded further: All of those people around a big ark in a semicircle meet and are part of something

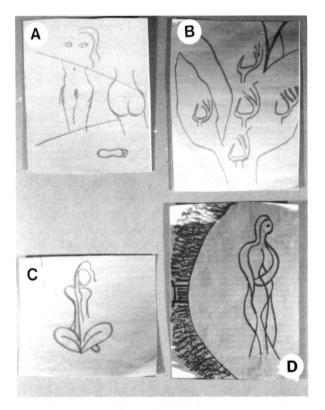

Figure 8-1.

bigger (Figure 8-1D). Again I was aware of eyes, as those in the picture stared out and searched to be taken in. Her drawings were like soft, sensual fragments reaching out to say, "Hold me."

The patient's representations of her body seemed segmented rather than forming a flowing whole, leading me to wonder if the holding she had received had been given by someone who was disengaged and unrelated. Putting those impressions together, I saw the religious force giving her a feeling of aliveness and superficial cohesion and, along with her eroticism, acting as a compensatory mechanism for her lack of the most basic of connections, that of the mother and child's early resonance.

Although Jan had not spoken of her mother, I sensed her presence in the room. My guess was that she was a brisk, hurried person, easily overwhelming to her child. The child who still dwelled within this patient was hungry for contact, while concurrently feeling frightened of being overwhelmed and controlled as she was by her mother. Those dual pulls caused her to fragment and become diffuse when intimate contact was offered. My initial musings were to be confirmed at a much later point in treatment.

At the same time as images of the mother permeated the atmosphere, a sense of her father crowded into the room with us, in spite of his having gone unmentioned by the patient. I suspected that he was the one who supplied physical contact and warmth in a nonverbal way, offering Jan some semblance of definition. That too was confirmed in later sessions.

In this brief description I have attempted to hint at the complex interaction of objective and subjective realities that create a psychological space between two people right from the beginning of therapy. Within that space past and present merge to create a unique mood and atmosphere. I experience the patient's inner representations of her past being born in the present. I sense, feel, and see the affects, moods, and attitudes originally connected to her past relationships as they are organized and represented in images and pictures that literally fill my office. Those representations speak of the me and you inside each of us that create our individual perceptions of the world and at the same time induce and shape the surrounding social world's response to each of us. The representations within any given patient make contact with the relationships I carry within me as a therapist.

Moving back to the case material, 2 years went by, and Jan and I struggled together with love, loss, and abandonment. There had been some important love relationships with men, but the same pattern continued: The men were wary, and as Jan in her hunger for love needed reassurance, they backed away.

As she shared her story, often with pain and depression, I felt both her helplessness and, paradoxically, a strange buoyancy. Depression did not seem to weigh her down. She occupied herself with endless tasks, as people came and went in her life. In reality, though, she lost no one as lovers turned into friends.

One day she came in and started in her typical fashion. I found myself not knowing what to say and suspecting that she was seeing me as far away. Not being sure what to do about it, I thought that I really needed to see her to get a better sense of what was going on, and consequently I asked her to draw a picture of both of us in the office. I stopped to wonder whether I was acting out an induced feeling. Was it my need for contact that I was experiencing or hers? It could well have been that my feelings of being shut out reflected an important affect Jan was communicating to me. Jan protested but then proceeded, as she said: "You will be very big and I will be very small. I don't draw very well and I just don't like to do it."

To my injunction not to judge it, to let it speak for itself, she replied, "I just can't make my drawing say what my inner image is." "Don't worry about that," I implored. "Let whatever is in come out." After she finished the drawing she said, "There, look, I told you; you are very big and I am very small. It is a very bad drawing—there is too much missing—it is very childlike" (Figure 8-2). "What's missing?" I asked. "All the details," she replied.

I suggested that she include all the things she'd like to have in, and she said she couldn't because she didn't have the artistic talent. She added that she would list them, though. "What I see missing are facial expressions and warmth in the eyes, strength and warmth in the arms, and the fear of passivity and receptivity."

I felt that now that she had written down the various aspects missing in her drawing, perhaps she had internalized enough

structure and definition to be ready to go on to the next step—
that of putting more definition into a drawing of herself.

She drew the next picture and stated that she was pleased
with it (Figure 8-3). There were still things missing, but there
were also important things included. I asked her once again to
list the things that were in the drawing as well as those that were
left out. She drew on one side of the page the things that were
in. First was the world *adamancy,* about which she said, "I don't
know if there even is such a word, but that's what I feel." Next
came eyes that were not drinking in, but were strong, looking

Figure 8-2.

defiant and determined and winning. What she put down as left out was "pressing lips."

Suddenly Jan became very tired, saying, "It's all too much for me." It was as though some strange presence had entered the room. I asked her what it felt like at that moment within herself, and she responded: "I feel my mother's eyes judging me, and I want to hide; I want to go away."

I thought back to her initial drawings of 2 years ago, the place with the eyes. I now had a better sense of them, for those

Figure 8-3.

eyes both drank in and became sharply critical. She ran from her mother's eyes. Jan explained: "It was pretty difficult with my mother, who was so strong-minded and strong-willed, always criticizing me. It was too much to combat her, so I went along, played, then went my own way. That's how I survived."

I suggested that she put that down, and as a bit more affect returned, I encouraged her to allow her secret self to be secret. She drew a quarter of the picture exposed, three-quarters with a line down the middle. "It's like a plane going through my body," she said, "and that's the part that's all mine, that nobody really sees" (Figure 8-4).

That session became a turning point in our treatment. We were both faced with the notion that she did not want to be seen for fear of being controlled and judged. The mother's presence was not only in the room but potentially in each of the relationships that abruptly terminated for one reason or another. For Jan the "bad mother" was well ensconced within her, constantly causing her to maintain an intensely private self. She was always hiding from the prying, judging eyes of Momma. She would end

Figure 8-4.

up re-creating the same hated relationship with the men in her life; she would control them while keeping them at a distance. She most likely chose men who were themselves fairly isolated, thereby supporting her defenses.

In terms of the transference/countertransference phenomenon, our sessions were filled with the struggle between Jan's need and wish for me to be a good mother, with the accompanying fear that I wouldn't be there, that I'd be the bad, prying, judgmental mother of her youth.

REBECCA

I vividly remember my first impressions of Rebecca. Her body was taut with tension. She was like a cat ready to spring out from the corner. With one sweep of her eyes she'd try to assess who was friend or foe. As she sat down, she pulled her chair farther away from me, indicating quite clearly that she was wary of close contact. Her voice was punctuated into tight sentences that spat out why she had come. She had been in treatment with several therapists for several years. Some she had liked, some she couldn't stand, and a few helped her. Now, she was panicked once again. She was in a Ph.D. psychology program, and everything seemed too much for her. She was worried about the field work, and intimidated by the instructors, and she felt very much alone. She was holding onto life by a thin thread. Amid protestations that she was drowning, she seemed to function very well: her grades were pretty good, she had many friends, and she was living with a man who was quite supportive.

Rebecca's description of her mother was that of Joan Crawford's character in the movie *Mommie Dearest*. Such adjectives as depressed, paranoid, angry, possessive, narcissistic, cruel came to mind as characterizing this woman Rebecca rarely got along with. Her father, on the other hand, was a rather weak and passive man. Compared to her mother, he was clearly less dangerous, and she could invest some love in him.

Four years into treatment Rebecca had finished graduate school and was functioning in a clinic where most of her patients were diagnosed as being borderline or having severe characterological conditions. She had invested strongly in a positive relationship with me that left her with overwhelming feelings of terror and desertion at vacation times. When I was gone, it was as though I did not exist. She had no image of me and seemingly could not remember who I was or what I was. She'd cling to substitute therapists and hope for the best. In September she was already girding herself for my next vacation. During that time her father, who now lived in California, became quite ill. He seemed to be approaching a kind of senile adjustment and was becoming less aware of her. Rebecca was finding it very hard to visit him.

She thought it was coincidental that she brought in material just then about how working with psychotherapeutic patients was just too much for her: They made too many demands on her and she simply couldn't maintain the kinds of limits she knew to be necessary in working with those kinds of clients.

With me she complained that she couldn't tell where I stood, that I was too noncommital, that she couldn't read me. That was in spite of the fact that I was fairly open and sharing with her. The image of the patient's father loomed oppressively in the room. He made a sad and pathetic picture, playing pitifully on other people's sympathy and looking for nurturance and support wherever he could get it. "He was always this way," Rebecca complained, "only now he's worse than ever."

It all seemed too much for her, as her impotence and rage overwhelmed her and she spat out: "What good is treatment? Everything remains the same!" In one session, after a typical litany of complaints about work, her progress in therapy, her inability to feel my presence, I asked her to draw a picture of the two of us. She agreed, commenting that drawing had always been something concrete, something she could see. She drew a big mouth and said that it was all that existed. "It's really my father's mouth," she said, then added, "and my hands are outside there, helping to hold him together" (Figure 8-5).

Then, as she drew a line going inside, she said: "I'm also a reflection of the inside. If I'm on the outside I'm disconnected and I'm punished and I will die. I have to face the fear that I'm going to be murdered or perhaps kill someone else."

I asked her to draw that picture, and what emerged was a

Doberman, "a killer and erratic, ready to kill at a moment's notice." A cocker spaniel was drawn, this one "warm, safe, constant,
but not very strong" (Figure 8-6). Strong or not, I commented
that this dog filled more space in the picture. She responded
that she was usually like that dog with her patients, until recently
when she'd started to fell cornered, and that she could kill them
all.

When I asked her why she'd put her feelings into a dog,
Rebecca related how she had had a dog as a child who had been
her special friend and ally. The recipient of warmth and safety,
he had been taken away from her because she developed aller-
gies. Next her thoughts jumped to my last summer vacation and

Figure 8-5.

her obsession with her supervisor's dog, an obsession that was strangely comforting.

With Rebecca's reconnecting with part of her nurturing past, she was filled with a calm and centeredness that lasted a couple of days until a supervisor shattered her peace by reactivating the terrorizing mother within her. New at the clinic, he demanded to know why some of her patients had terminated at the clinic and followed Rebecca into private practice. She again felt frightened for her very being.

In trying to make sense out of it all I asked her to remember her first picture with its ambiguity as to whether it was me or her father. She responded "That's how it is with my father; with you, it's like . . ." and started to draw. "It's like a breast, and I am like a baby who is blind and cannot get to the nipple (Figure 8-7). My dog could reach out and come to me. He could smell me out, but with my parents I had to sit helplessly and impotently. No one reached out to me." Both of us began to understand why art had become so important to her: it gave her an opportunity to see, to touch, to smell what was around her. My hope was that with those recognitions she could now come out of her

Figure 8-6.

blinded psychic existence, but she continued to wait for me to reach out to her. She still felt there was no help, that she was all by herself in her existential state of blindness and aloneness. The pictures, however, became a mirror for her internal existence, and together we shared her terror, her anger, and her upset.

She came to see how rarely she let anyone come inside her for fear of being possessed. Anyone coming close was the equivalent of an act of possession. I wondered aloud if that always had to be the case. Could she take someone inside without being possessed? It was very clear that our next line of work was to be an investigation into how two people could be close while being separate; how to take someone in and still preserve the core of oneself.

Meanwhile, the picture of the angry, aggressive dog versus the sweet, warm, oral, incorporative dog became important symbols for Rebecca in terms of integrating the various levels of her hunger. Such questions emerged as: Could warmth and anger be integrated in one person? Would anger necessarily destroy?

In our next session Rebecca began by reviewing material of

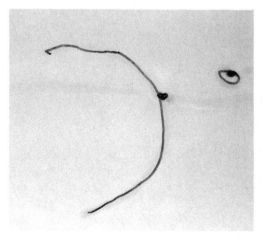

Figure 8-7.

the last two sessions and was very excited about it. She described how she'd had particular difficulty in reading or taking in anything, and the importance of her dog in her life. Her childhood dog had really been an important friend to her. In fact, she felt unable to get the same sense of support—or touching—anywhere else. She spoke of how she wanted very much to be touched, to feel connections; meanwhile she sat holding her hands tightly clenched together.

I asked whether it would be possible for me to trace her hands, and she agreed under the proviso that she could hold them together. I traced the hands, then asked if I could do it again with the two hands spread separately on the paper (Figure 8-8). She did that but felt quite frightened about the closeness of the contact, saying that it felt "awful, frightening."

"How would it feel," I asked, "if I bring in my dog?" The

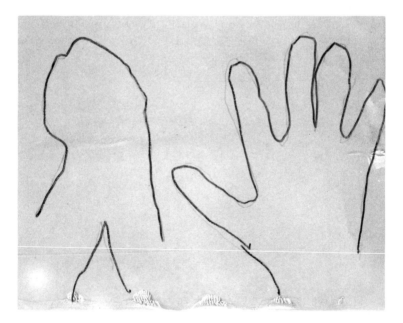

Figure 8-8.

idea clearly intrigued her. She knew the dog's name, Paddington, and was rather fond of him. I called him, he bounded in, and immediately went to sit next to Rebecca. "You see," she said, "if you were able to lick me like this dog does, we'd have no trouble making contact." We laughed, but then as she started to pet the dog, she broke into tears and began to cry painfully. Unable to describe why, she communicated the depth of her pain to me. The unspoken message was clear, at least to me: If she could only get this contact from her parents, what a different life it would have been. Interestingly, the patient complained during the session that she could not read the material that would help her be a better therapist. Now the patient all but made the connection that the isolation of her early world did indeed impair some of her ability to understand her outer reality verbally and conceptually.

When I later told her I was going to use part of her material as part of an article or perhaps even part of a book, she looked at me rather warily. I described the purpose and pointed out that I would first show the material to her for her approval, to which she said, "Oh, you are going to teach me how to read!"

Thus, we had created a further extension of the mirroring transference. Here, as with Jan, we see the split of the good and bad mother and the transferential coloring that brought to sessions. On the one hand, there was the image of the therapist as the good breast, but concurrently Rebecca could not reach out as images of her impotent father and terrorizing introjected mother flooded her.

As she saw parts of herself mirrored back nonverbally and verbally in the artwork and the therapeutic relationship, pieces of her world became more organized. She internalized a more integrated image, and with that, associated ego skills improved, she felt less lonely, and was generally better able to cope.

BOB

From the beginning Bob's upper torso was in a tight, neuromuscular vise. Medication didn't help, he could hardly sleep,

and a series of bioenergetic sessions were of temporary help at
best.

Bob came from a family of nine children living in a small
town out West. His father was a well-respected doctor whose
credo was that of achievement and success. The children followed
in their father's footsteps and also were successful. Bob's mother
had wanted him to become a doctor. He tried, but the language
of medicine didn't speak to him, whereas that of art exerted a
strong pull.

In June of our second year of treatment Bob had begun to
relax and accept the support of the therapeutic relationship. With
my vacation he returned to his former tight, pained existence.
Once again the therapy atmosphere reminded him of all the
constriction and isolation he had felt years ago when his parents
hadn't been there to hold him or to give him the help and support
he needed.

Bob recognized that he was angry, but he couldn't express
his feelings. He tried hard to deal with this constriction but only
ended up in a tight obsessional, ruminative knot. He just couldn't
feel that I was on his side any longer.

He came in one session again complaining of the enormous
pain in his back, and I asked him to visualize the pain and see
who was living there. His image was that of an embryo all curled
up. The isolation of that embryo, as he described it, was very
poignant. I wondered out loud what it would take for him to
feel once again that I was supporting him. Could he visualize
that experience, I asked. "Only with difficulty," he responded.
"You go away for your summers, and it's very hard for me to
feel that you're really here behind me. I know I don't have any
real right to make demands on anyone." Then the image of his
mother came to him, that of a woman all too busy to spend too
much time with any one child. He then said: "If I am to get help,
it is only temporary, and that is particularly true of you."

He then spoke about the double bind of support. If one did
get support it always came with a catch: that he'd have to live
up to expectations, be a good patient, listen, and try to take the
therapist's advice. As was true of so much of his life, he seethed
with unexpressed anger while trying to do what was expected
of him.

I requested that perhaps he should try to draw some of the significant phases of what we had talked about in the session and gave him the assignment of drawing the following pictures: (a) Art [refers to the therapist, Art Robbins] supporting my back; (b) I take Art along with me; (c) Art goes away for the summer and my feelings about it; (d) I am curled up in my chest; (e) I have no right to make demands of my mother; (f) if I am going to get help, it is only temporary from Art, for it ultimately means desertion; (g) if I can get Art's support, he will make demands on me to be a good patient; (h) at best Art is but a lonely trip; (i) I see my family and I see Art: how they are different and how they are the same.

When he came back, he said it took the whole weekend to get over his resentment of doing anything for me. He finally realized that it was for his own good, and with much underlying annoyance and resistance, he began to draw.

He was fairly pleased with the results, even proud, as he

Figure 8-9.

condensed the pictures and showed me his work. The first picture had to do with support (Figure 8-9). It was of a sad inward person reconciled, trying to allow expectations, but not believing that he could or would get support. It was interesting that the lower part of his body was missing. That became a theme running throughout his drawings. As he viewed me in the drawing, he described me as rather serious, and the space between us as "that of waiting." He tried to draw my holding him, yet his own body refused the physical invitation. Bob had great trouble responding to that image; it was so unreal to him. He couldn't even imagine the feelings he would have in such a situation. His faces were all looking poignant, sad, inward, and downward.

The second drawing was called "Think of Art around me." He drew a picture of me in a cart, and I thought it interesting that he saw himself carrying me around (Figure 8-10). Was I a burden, I wondered out loud, since I seemed to be standing there resistant while Bob stiffly carried the handle of his cart.

Figure 8-10.

In the third picture, I was on a conveyer belt along with other important people in his life (Figure 8-11). Again he depicted himself in the passive position, waiting expectantly. "My father was a doctor. I was never truly a patient of his; perhaps if I were really sick I'd get the care I wanted. I do get momentary relief from this belief, but I am always back smack in the same place needing to be protected. It's too hard to get around the barrier, even in fantasy." He looked again and noted that the way the conveyer belt went on, I might just pass him by. There were bars there, and all he could do was to wait passively.

I said nothing as he described his lot in life and went on to his next picture (Figure 8-12). Here he was locked, strapped, and secured to a barrier. He acknowledged our separateness and the emotional tone of his family. He depicted himself as fat and

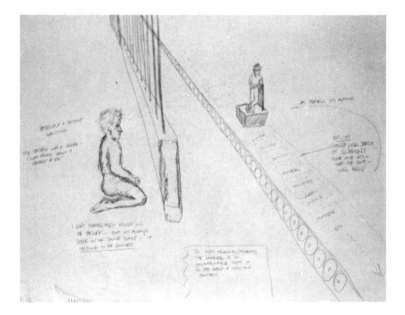

Figure 8-11.

in pain. We were both sitting passively in a stand-off. I was wait-ing.

His last picture further amplified his dilemma (Figure 8-13). Again his feet were not connected to the ground. The bottom half of his body was barely drawn; the top was in a cloudlike mass with eyes all around; my eyes in glasses also were included. "This is how I see my family, and this is how I see Arthur," he stated. "Everyone is watching me and the choices I make. One choice is the do-gooder-for-others as a clean, white, sparkling pan, and that's the place I've always chosen. The other part is messy—the place I've never chosen. It's unknown and maybe even exciting."

I reflected that it was difficult for anyone to move sur-rounded by judgment and questioned if he could now imagine me in a more supportive position. Could I stand behind his de-cision-making ability, I queried. Although he wasn't sure he could do that, at least the whole issue surrounding my support was out in the open. I was now a member of his family, and that

Figure 8-12.

was a beginning in unraveling his isolation from any affirmative force inside him.

For both of us art became a transitional space where Bob could reclaim his "eyes" that connected a self to an inner and outer reality. I suspected that to make that connection we probably would need to immerse ourselves in the mess of his instinctual life. I hoped that together we would discover that disorder could lead to a regeneration of the self with new possibilities and creations rather than a feeling of despair and badness.

As Bob investigated the transference, he began to see how much I was a part of his family's world. Through the drawings a map of Bob's internal world emerged where we may in the future be able to explore different trial adaptations with key figures in his life. I hoped that Bob would find the courage to trust me once more through the sharing and creating of his internal

Figure 8-13.

reality. Where the battle for self-affirmation was once lost, the art showed promise of being a means to reach out to Bob.

Let's take a look at the meaning of art within the transference/countertransference context. Here drawings of his passivity became an active form of protest. The active interest of the patient's art expression by the therapist was in sharp contrast to his parents, which facilitated a mirror transference. Here, intermixed with the tone of sadness and despair, was the real relationship affirming his right to be. It was hoped that that involvement would create a nexus for the repair of the lost ego ideal so crucial in the building of a more adequate masculine identification. Thus, with the support of the therapist Bob's instinctive life might evolve from a negative, passive, witholding attitude to one of an aggressive, sexual reaching out to life.

SUMMARY

There are a number of principles implicit in my treatment of those three patients that are intimately intertwined with the transference/countertransference relationships. I'd like to list them in order to give the reader a clearer picture of the context into which transference/countertransference phenomena fit.

1.   As therapists, we constantly create and evolve structures that organize the energy in the therapeutic relationship. Those structures, or holding environments, provide the framework for symbolic communications. In spite of the core of schizoid loneliness in all three patients, the outer constellations, ranging from hysteria to paranoia and depression, colored the tones of the sessions and called for very different kinds of intervention.

2.   This holding environment encompasses both verbal and nonverbal art communications. The structures are presented on both levels, with an ongoing therapeutic interplay between them. As has been mentioned in earlier sections of this book, the art relationship sometimes supports, sometimes contradicts, sometimes enlarges the verbal one, but it always provides useful information.

3.   An extension of that principle holds that the aesthetic issues of patients offer clues to therapeutic interventions, which is well exemplified in the three cited cases. In Jan's drawing there was a lack of details and an internal vagueness to her images that offered new possibilities for exploration. Rebecca's two dogs, one hostile aggressive, the other oral incorporative, indicated a need for integration. Finally, in Bob's drawings there was an ongoing theme of his lower body being depicted amorphous and poorly grounded. That issue became an important part of our ongoing therapeutic interaction.

4.   The goal of the interplay between the art and "real" therapeutic relationship is to facilitate a greater perceptual and affective differentiation between past and present realities. Jan did, in fact, move from more vagueness to more definition; Rebecca for the first time internalized a sense of nurturance and calm; and Bob started to differentiate between therapist and family support.

5.   Both patient and therapist move back and forth from the art form to the relationship. A fabric is then woven between both parties that is created from the patient's developmental level and the transference/countertransference interplay. For all three case illustrations, clear, defined, supportive relationships were extremely useful in dealing with an inner sense of aloneness.

The artwork often became a container for the transference/ countertransference material. Art also provided a space for patients to master a degree of control while taking steps toward greater intimacy in treatment.

6.   For all three patients the work was reparative, developmental, and transferential in nature. For Jan, issues of attachment as well as fear of intrusion led her to create a secret self that became one of the main issues under investigation. Her movement in and out of intimacy and attachment were typical of this level of developmental organization. Where Jan needed the space to uncover her secret self, Rebecca was like a blind baby looking for the breast, requiring an active stance by the therapist to clarify, define, and confront the various facets of her self within the confines of a safe environment.

Bob presented a strong need for internalizing a paternal

ego ideal that would support and encourage him to move out into the world and embrace it. Art, then, became a transitional object to repair a feeling of abandonment and despair.

7.   As therapists, we move along multiple levels of consciousness to facilitate different levels of structure and organization. Yet like all artists, we must be in charge of our discipline. Our tools include both developmental theory and a sensitivity to aesthetic expression. That includes an understanding of ego organization. Thus, Rebecca often required a defined, clear structure that could facilitate a connected exploration of her life. Bob required a supportive freedom to play with his instincts to regain ego mastery. Jan had to make an active choice to hide or expose in order to become more cohesively defined.

8.   Patient's communications can be viewed within a context of gestalt organization. Each part of the patient/therapist dialogue can potentially be part of the total gestalt. Here, we view communications in their totality, while at the same time we attempt to understand their individual components. By offering structures we try to integrate parts of our own unconscious with an understanding of the case to promote greater integrations of self-expressions. Essentially, the therapist's and patient's communications are like two parts of a diptych, each lending richness to the other, each facilitating a closure of a formerly incomplete dialogue.

In summary, art forms are the containers and frames for the therapeutic interplay of transference/countertransference interactions. As such, they are extremely important extensions of the transference that provide safe structures within which to explore the painful effects of nothingness and abandonment. Here we observe the uniqueness of the art therapeutic relationship: externalizing, containing, reorganizing, and offering the patient and therapist the opportunity to share a common reality.

Chapter 9

REGENERATION OF THE POTENTIAL LIFE SPACE OF THE ANTITHERAPEUTIC PATIENT

I'd like to talk about a long-standing member of my case load who defies neat diagnostic categories. Sometimes referred to as a "false self" personality, this patient is one who ostensibly functions in society at a fairly high level but fails to establish more than emotionally shallow relationships. He can characteristically go through several courses of therapy without apparent benefit. As frustratingly antitherapeutic as this patient may appear, he can be reached and worked with effectively in therapy if the therapist incorporates a sound theoretical framework and a dynamic treatment approach.

In the consultation room a picture of seeming contradictions presents itself. This patient may project a sense of vitality and busyness, often appearing compulsive as he works hard, often over long hours, exhibiting an endless supply of energy. To the outside world this individual presents a fairly good accounting of himself. With many acquaintances, he is often respected and well-liked and can be charming when the situation demands such behavior. There is a darker side to all that, however. Even when present and listening, he doesn't seem to hear, being intent on preparations to move on to something else. This busyness is, in fact, a necessity, for he cannot tolerate being emotionally connected to any one person for any length of time.

His inability to maintain an emotional connection becomes apparent under the impact of the therapeutic relationship. What emerges is a restricted, depressing picture as endless repetitions and reportings of days' events are presented. There is a quality of impoverishment to this patient's communications due to the paucity of ideas, meaningful symbols, associations, or connections between past and present. Dreams are few, and fantasy is on the superficial side. All of this creates a chasm between the patient and therapist that widens and deepens as the patient, in a polite, reasonable, insidious way, destroys any attempt on the part of the therapist to make connections or give meaning to the communications. This undermining often evidences itself as apparent agreement with observations of the therapist while the patient himself remains consistently untouched and cut off from emotional content. Regardless of the degree of empathy, confrontation, or explanation, the therapist's interventions make very little difference.

What the therapist comes to feel reflects the transference/countertransference phenomenon that is so much a part of indepth therapy. The sense of static hopelessness in the sessions mirrors the patient's sense of futility at being cut off, of nothing happening, and of impotence to effect change. Sadness and loneliness emanate on a somatic level in spite of the lack of affect or words spoken. The patient has recreated his early family situation in this transference/countertransference relationship. It becomes clear how alone and cut off the patient must have felt as the therapist registers his own sense of disconnection, despair, and impotence to make change happen in relation to this patient. It dawns on the therapist that this is like all of the other courses of therapy the patient has pursued where nothing has happened. Finally, the therapist develops a deep sense of guilt at being party to such a futile venture.

Bion (1977) and Winnicott (1971) describe these patients as being afflicted with a deep sense of ego castration and as possessing a "false self" personality, respectively. Bion's expression (1977) comes from his observation that for such patients there is very little meaning or association between past events and present experiences. He also sees a violent splitting off of meaningful inner object worlds and instinctual roots as characteristic. Winnicott more clearly addresses the causal aspect of this clinical picture in postulating inadequate parenting experiences in the childhoods of such individuals.

Winnicott presents the evolution of the "false self" personality in terms we've briefly looked at before in discussing more normal development. The concepts of "primary space" and "primary creativity" take on a specific coloration as they are reflected in our patient. Primary creativity is part of the earliest mother/infant relationship, named for the sense the neonate is thought to have of creating what he needs because the mother's attunement is so perfect. The dyad, in essence, creates a world, or a space, between and including themselves where the mother gives order and cohesion to the massive stimuli bombarding the baby. She does that through the looking, cooing, rocking, playing, physical caring that comprises the newborn's world.

Over time the play and interactions in this "potential space" help the baby to differentiate his own unique sense of self from "other." It is also here where confidence in the mother's dependability is taken in and evolves into self-esteem, trust, and a more general confidence in the environment. Separation is made easier by the filling in of the space with playing, symbols, and what eventually will add up to a cultural life.

If the mother has failed to be dependable, whether because she is intrusive, unrelated, dissociated, or simply not present, the lack of adaptation is experienced by the baby as an impingement, in the sense that his continuity of being has been violently interrupted. The infant does not develop trust in the environment, does not have the good mothering experience to internalize as self-esteem, and in self-defense buries, or splits off, his budding sense of self. Henceforth, he will studiously adapt and comply with his environment, but lacking the earliest reliable connection with mother, he will fail to build bridges with others. Symbolic experiences also will go under cover, with psyche and soma splitting to go their separate ways.

Evidence of this embedding of symbols is often seen in the body. Organs may complain, weep, or occasionally erupt in either psychosomatic or hypochondriacal frenzy. The body becomes the messenger. The energy and despair that emanate from such patients are simply two components of an aura of seething bodily communications.

Several factors make this kind of patient a formidable challenge to any therapist. Aside from a deep hatred and fear of a regeneration of relatedness that would cause him to reexperience painfully deep loss, the "false self" personality also uses words in a way that work against the therapeutic process. The patient is basically unable to decode, feel, or experience what his body is saying because psyche and soma are so isolated from one another. Consequently, kinesthetic experiences are on the shallow side. Furthermore, because words do not transcend linear logic, they cannot move into the world of primary process where fantasy and symbols reign; and time, space, and inner representations merge, flow, and create their own truth and structure. Without any awareness of his destructiveness, anger, wish to mess or mar, the patient will deliver verbal communications that become, in essence, fecalized deposits placed at the therapist's doorstep for disposal. As you will see in the case of Bob, this choice of words is not accidental.

In light of these considerations, it is understandable how Joyce McDougall (1980), among others, has come to the conclusion from her work with these patients that mirroring, reflecting, offering one's self as a steady, reliable object in whom these patients can invest is simply not enough in and of itself to promote long-term reorganization. What is needed is to engage the patient in such a way that there can be a regeneration of the potential life space that went awry in infancy. The patient must discover his own meaningful symbols that have a sensory and bodily connection and will serve to link past to present. As Piaget (1936) demonstrated, abstraction and symbolization evolve from the baby's earliest actions and reactions on a sensorimotor level from birth to about 2 years of age; therefore, meaning must first be framed through concrete forms of communication. The use of art materials with Winnicott's formulations of play as that which helps create and define space, self, and other combine to form a good means to approach therapy and help create meaning for these patients.

More specifically, clay can be an excellent medium with

which to work in this context. Its qualities of being fluid, manageable, and fast moving appeal to the patient's prevalent needs to be in control and to keep busy. At the same time clay tends to evoke sensations and feelings associated with the budding body ego. For this patient to be truly connected to his body and evolve through Piaget's sensorimotor stage to more abstract ways of thinking, he must first work through the early issues organized around bowel control, including mess, rage, expulsion, control, product formation, and creation.

A word of caution is to be added here. Clay is not in and of itself a pat answer or magic formula for working with these patients. The formidable therapeutic issues to be worked through will trigger the same defense and resistance against meaning as will a straight verbal approach. The advantages of the art medium, however, are twofold. First, words are less evocative of play than is a nonverbal medium, so clay can become an invitation to play or a means through which the patient can learn to play. At the same time, play with clay gives the therapist a medium through which to deal with his own countertransference reactions. If willing to participate and interact with the patient through play, the therapist can both aid the patient's understanding of communication through reflecting back and help the patient see and feel the inner world of the therapist as he attempts to contain and organize his own countertransference experiences in the therapeutic interaction. That interplay of concrete and symbolic reactions and interactions becomes the focal point for a shared reality and regeneration of a potential life space.

The following case vignettes of Bob, Ellen, and Tom will illustrate some of the particular technical issues present in regenerating Winnicott's potential space with the antitherapeutic patient.

CASE 1

Bob had been in treatment for approximately a year and a half on a once-a-week basis in both individual and group therapy when this was written. Previously he had seen seven other therapists of various theoretical persuasions. Each course of therapy ended with very little success. Characteristically, he would complain in treatment of no change.

His background was a fairly deprived one. Mother, a card player and a gambler, spent most of her time away from the children, and when she was home was fairly self-involved with her own pursuits and interests. At the age of forty she started to deteriorate physically. She withdrew more severely into herself and complained endlessly about one physical disorder or another. The father, who diligently worked in his store seven days a week, was described by the patient as well-meaning but very passive and also involved in his own particular affairs.

The patient was bitter and angry about his background. He felt deprived, unloved, and uncared for. In spite of those limitations he made his own way in the world carrying the atmosphere of his home wherever he traveled. That was especially true in therapy. Nothing was very good. He complained endlessly and seemed to be living out an identification with his mother in her later hypochondriacal years. Bob felt I was a good therapist even though I was impotent in my efforts to help him. There was a pointless quality to the sessions, yet the patient would come on time and seem to value them.

Events were reported in a routine, pointless tone. I attempted to investigate some of the patient's feelings about his past and to use my induced reactions as a point of reference. I found my own boredom covered a rage that was most often a mirroring of Bob's early experiences of his family. I tried to elicit dreams, but characteristically, Bob presented few, and those that did emerge had a flat, stereotyped quality. Nothing seemed to work.

Endlessly, Bob would drone on about the impotence of treatment and the inability of any therapist to help him. Endlessly he'd complain about the lack of any real social relationships in his life while he did very little to change this condition. Finally I suggested that we work with clay and was met with a suspicious look. Bob clearly wondered what good this new tack could produce. His first response to clay was to tear the material into small bits and to point out to me that this reflected his attitude toward everything. There were random bits and pieces that ended up nowhere. I looked at the display in front of me as he laid it out and agreed with him that it looked like a pile of small turds. He fingered the remaining clay as he started to talk about his recent involvement in a tennis game and how he saw himself improving. Even then, he attacked himself as he wondered aloud whether he was really good enough and was getting the most out of his tennis lesson.

As he started to talk more to me about his experience playing tennis, he started to rub the clay and turn it into a cylinder. Slowly he squared it off. He looked at it suddenly and said, "You know, this reminds me of a loaf of bread." I smiled and said, "You know, it is often referred to as the staff of life." He looked at me and shrugged his shoulders, remaining silent until the end of the session.

We met the next time in a group session. As the group members started to talk about some important experiences in their backgrounds, particularly ones regarding their mothers, the patient spoke of the only meaningful experience he could remember with his mother. It turned out she was a very good cook, although even here she continuously complained and didn't seem to get too much satisfaction out of it. I reminded him of the bread he had made in the session before. "Yes," he said, "when I go out to eat, I love bread. I just can't get enough of it. Bread is something that is so important to me." I then reminded the patient of how often he brought up the subject of restaurants and would offer me names of good eating places in the New York area. I related to the rest of the group about our experience in individual sessions, saying that perhaps this was one of our most meaningful forms of exchange. The patient smiled broadly, realizing that at some level there was a very important link between the bread, his mother, and our own particular form of communication. The beginning of a bridge between us was made, and a real exchange regarding primary symbolism was being converted into a secondary process communication as the meaningless bits and pieces of fecal mass gave way to the symbol of the staff of life, the bread that was shaped into a loaf.

I want to reemphasize the importance of Bob's taking the meaningless mess and converting it into a concrete visual communication so his anger and destructiveness could be accepted and evolve into the meaningful symbol of bread. To say it in a slightly different way, the verbal antitherapeutic level was converted into a nonverbal level of tactile play and expression. Clay became a vehicle for Bob's reconnection with somatic representation. Being first concrete, he could finally move on to the symbolic expression of bread, the staff of life.

CASE 2

Ellen was a thirty-five-year-old woman, twice divorced and was involved in a legal separation from her third husband at the time of this writing. She had been in treatment on a once-a-week basis for approximately 1 year. In spite of being a very bright woman, Ellen showed an impoverishment of ideas and affect. Typically, she spoke in a flat, monotonous voice as she complained about her loneliness and the wish to regain her husband and to repair her marriage. As was true with Bob, sessions were repetitious, and boredom hung in the air.

Eventually, out of a desperate need to make some kind of meaningful contact, I introduced the medium of clay to our relationship. She approached the idea with some distaste and made faces at the thought of getting herself dirty and messy. After some encouragement, however, she started to work with the material with little enthusiasm or involvement. Interestingly, as soon as she made an image she would destroy it, rather than complete any form or shape. This process went on through the entire session. As I pointed this process out to her, it occurred to her that working with clay or doing anything like that reminded her of her childhood and the feeling she had had that her mother, a psychologist, could read her mind when Ellen would do a drawing. She readily admitted that she had resented that intrusion, and now she really didn't want me to see anything about her. It was clear that Ellen's symbolic impoverishment and flat affect had originally been used to protect herself against her mother's invasions. I wondered out loud what we could do about this. She suggested I work with clay as well, and I readily agreed.

In the next session she went back to the clay and asked me to participate along with her. As she started to work on her piece, she slyly looked over to watch me work with my clay. Slowly a dinosaur emerged, which I labeled "Danny the Dinosaur." She asked me about it, and I told her about Danny the Dinosaur, who had a big intrusive neck and seemed to always stick his nose into places where he had no business. He was a friendly enough dinosaur, though, I added. Ellen laughed, but at the same time she was somewhat suspicious of the way I spoke to her. She said I spoke to her like a child, and she couldn't quite decide whether she liked it or not. I asked her about her piece of work, and she said it was just an abstract piece of something flowing in the wind. I questioned aloud how involved she really was in the piece, to which she responded that she was doing it for me. "I always do things for people," she said, "but this has very little meaning for me." When questioned why she really did it, she said it was to please me. In response I told her that Danny the Dinosaur was really for me, that I was involved in it. I commented that Danny reminded me a good deal of my background, where intrusion and people butting in were an important part of my past relationships. I shared that sculpting had always been a form of release for me, for I found in this medium a place where I could be myself. Ellen listened to me with a good deal of interest.

In the next session Ellen requested that we go back to clay. This time she seemed much more involved in her clay work. Out of it evolved an abstract work of mother and child. She looked at the piece and said that as much as she attempted to put the child in, all that she could do was the mother. She quickly saw that the mother figure that she had created closely reflected her own experience. It was interesting that the figure had a strong back but a very weak front, and Ellen made a poignant comment about that. "It's like the front really can't support her as she seems very weak and bent over. There's a big hole inside of her and as much as I want to put a child there, a child really doesn't seem to belong." She then turned to me and asked me about my work. I showed her the face I had created rather quickly and she noted that it looked all marred. I commented that I felt pretty mushed over from the day's events. I had been stuck on the train and felt rushed and irritated by all the delays in getting to my office. She laughed as we shared and looked at each other's clay pieces.

For the first time the patient was able to truly involve herself in working through a meaningful symbol. Slowly a space was developing where we could share a reality that existed between us. Both of us had viewed her defensive operations and a corrective solution had been advanced by the patient. Instead of feeling invaded, which required the severe defenses of denial and dissociation, the patient participated in now symbolic, now verbal play with the therapist. Instead of meaningless gifts, a real sharing and joining was generated.

CASE 3

My final case is that of a baker, Tom, who was in his third year of treatment and for whom there had been a number of significant changes. In spite of those changes, however, there remained a frenetic quality to his behavior. He couldn't really sit still or stay in one place, which was reflected in treatment and in his relationships.

In our sessions Tom rarely talked about his past, but from what sparse information did emerge, a lonely, emotionally deprived picture was presented. Both of Tom's parents spent long hours in the bakery, which was characterized by the patient as a place of drudgery and boredom. Tom was left with a variety of substitute parents, all of whom were equally inadequate. For his mostly absent parents he felt little respect or regard. He saw them as drudges who cared little for life and were consumed with the business of making money. Angry, defiant, and disconnected, Tom seemed to float through life from one relationship to another.

Although essentially homosexual in life-style, Tom married and cast his wife in the role of a strong protective barrier against a frightening world. After 6 years of marriage his restlessness and disconnection erupted, and a yearning for something unclear and missing pushed Tom into treatment. Shortly thereafter, he was able to leave his unhappy marriage and find a homosexual lover with whom he lived and from whom he derived a good deal of satisfaction. In spite of that Tom continued to seek out one homosexual experience after another. He seemed to have a number of acquaintances, all of whom found him quite charming and winning.

In therapy Tom's communications were chatty and devoid of any real meaning. He could tell me little about his love affair or other important relationships and couldn't relate fantasies or dreams. He nevertheless maintained that he felt supported by the therapist, helped, and related to. He said he looked forward to seeing me, but once present would constantly look at the clock as he waited for the time to be over.

Again, after an unproductive period of time, I suggested we work in clay. Tom's response was one of anxiety. "Is this something new?" he cautiously asked. After reassurance we started to work. Tom's hands trembled. He looked at them and wondered out loud why he was shaking all over. In spite of his trepidation he proceeded to struggle with the clay. We talked about his anxiety. What came out was a vague, ill-defined fear of my judging his work. He started to work on a rose and put together the individual petals. Finally, with a good deal of struggle, he completed his work and presented it to me.

He admired his figure with pleasure. Then rather abruptly he said, "You know, what I really wanted to do was to make a penis, but I felt too ashamed of this." Rarely had this man reacted with such feeling or produced such depth of meaning.

Although all that Tom could show at that point was the soft, delicate, pliable part of himself in graphic form, we both now knew that behind that was a phallic power of which he was ashamed. Without a father whom he could respect and a sensitive, caring mother to have fostered early self-esteem and confidence, Tom had been driven to compulsive acting out in numerous gay alliances. As his hands had trembled before him, he had been able to grapple with the fact that he could speak through creation, not only action. In a concrete representative form his defenses were captured in operation, but more important, he transcended impulsive acting out to symbolize, to convert to representational thought, to be able to share that material with an authority figure.

Treatment could now take on a deeper and more profound course because a bridge—or transitional space, if you will—had been created with which to work. It was clear as we looked at the clay rose that someday the flower would be combined with the strong root of male identification.

In each of those cases the therapist was able to observe

through concrete representational form character defenses in operation. Bob showed his need to turn everything into meaningless feces as a means to identify with his mother but at the same time hide his deep craving for a feeding, nourishing contact with her. Ellen's superficial compliance masked her fears of self-expression and resentment at intrusion. Tom needed to face the early anxiety of representing his experiences in symbolic form, risking the exposure that reawakened infancy fears of annihilation.

Those defenses reflected deficits in early supportive, nourishing relationships, without which these patients hadn't the "stuff" to build strong, integrated, senses of themselves. Bob's mothering experience was one of emotional unavailability, Ellen's of intrusiveness, Tom's of actual absence. Because their environments were hostile to the development of trust and confidence, their true "selves" were so deeply embedded in protective adaptations to their surroundings that none of those patients were in touch with themselves. Words had simply become integral parts of their masterful adaptive systems and rendered therapy ineffective.

What was necessary was to hook into the patients on a more primitive, concrete level and, through play, to create transitional bridges, which in turn fostered symbolization. Having discovered their symbols, the patients could then reconvert, or shape, them in words in order to integrate them into the personality and convert the false self into a solid, authentic self.

Chapter 10

A STUDY IN THE AESTHETICS OF PAIN, RAGE, LOSS, AND REINTEGRATION

John has leukemia and very much wants wants to live. We cannot assess the extent to which psychological etiology was a contributing factor to his medical condition, but he does present a classical background picture of the typical cancer patient: early loss compounded by a later loss, housed in a basic depressed personality of hopelessness and helplessness. The background of this patient presents an interesting insight into both the possibilities and limitations of utilizing art forms as means of healing. Neither John nor I maintain any illusions that psychotherapy will rescue him from his illness. Our efforts have been directed at improving his quality of life and affording him every opportunity to mobilize the healthy forces within his personality to combat disease. You will see how John came to understand the extent to which he created a self-fulfilling prophecy.

Much of section I has previously been published as part of a larger article entitled "A Creative Arts Approach to Therapy" (Robbins, 1984). It concentrates on organizing the case as it developed, as well as demonstrating the use and interplay of three modalities in working through a segment of treatment. Section

II reflects a subsequent period in treatment and further refines the relationship of aesthetics and this patient's inner world.

John's case is demonstrative of the difference between art as a medium of healing versus therapy. As a jazz pianist for whom music was the most pervasive force from adolescence onward, John drew on the deep, soulful rhythms that characterized his work for sustenance and fulfillment. In music he felt free and powerful. In music he also found a safe refuge, a place where buried affects could find expression without becoming frighteningly conscious or integrated with comprehension. Music served the paradoxical purposes of both connecting him to others while protecting him from them. What his music couldn't do was the job of therapy. As long as it served to split affect from awareness, John's music couldn't help reorganize the pathological structures within his personality. In treatment, however, music could be integrated with the real therapeutic relationship to become a transitional bridge between the inexplicable rhythms of his earlier life and his conscious. Art exercises served as a cognitive frame in which to organize the deep penetrating notes, while words ultimately allowed him to define consciously who and what he is.

I.

I vividly remember my initial impression of John. Thin and gaunt, his hair was prematurely gray, his face ashen, and his chest sunken in. There was a medicinal odor that clung to him and was repulsive. Only thirty-two, he looked much older; yet as I looked more closely, a boyish quality emerged with the shy smile that came and went from his face.

John was articulate and forthright in discussing his problems. The ostensible reason for entering treatment was a stormy and dissatisfying marriage. Married 6 years before to a black woman his own age, John had trouble communicating with and trusting his wife, as she did in return. A polarized cycle repeated itself so that when one wanted to be close, the other wanted distance. Even their preferred life-styles were radically different. John was a musician and teacher who was satisfied with his lot and didn't care that he earned very little money. His wife, on the other hand, wanted a middle-class existence. She exerted pressure on John to go out and earn more, since they had an agreement to each contribute 50%, and she felt her life-style was limited.

Her demands were in direct conflict with the enormous amount of time and energy John wanted to put into his musical work. As a concession to his wife, he started driving a cab two nights a week to earn more money, but he resented the drain and frustration that involved, especially after 5 or 6 hours of practicing his music. His wife also wanted to adopt a child, which John felt jeopardized his career.

I soon learned that the medicinal odor John emitted was the medication that was prescribed for tuberculosis. Although it was no longer in an active state, the disease was still being treated and would require additional medication for at least another 6 months.

The chief conflict as the patient saw it was whether or not to stay with his wife or perhaps to change his sexual orientation and enter the gay world. He was frightened about being homosexual, and yet at the same time he was intrigued by the kind of intimate sensuous contact that gay life afforded. That intimacy had been impossible to obtain in the sexual relationship he had with his wife. She simply didn't excite him.

John's history emerged as follows. John remembered very little about his mother, who died of breast cancer when he was seven; but he had been told that she was powerful, outgoing, and that he was close to her. When she died, his father, a rather withdrawn, quiet person, couldn't handle his son's emotional difficulties in the aftermath of the mother's death. John's father sent out strong nonverbal messages to leave him alone; he was having trouble coping as it was. It was easy to see how John came to feel cut off from and disappointed in his father.

He and his brother, a few years older, engaged in sex play when John was nine. That was soon discontinued, and the brothers drifted apart; but at twelve or thirteen John participated in sex play with a close black male friend. John never ceased to have strong sexual fantasies and longings for this relationship.

Four years ago John's wife required a hysterectomy. While she was in the hospital, John enjoyed a brief homosexual encounter in which he managed to lose her wedding ring. He immediately confessed the entire incident to this wife, further increasing the deterioration of the marriage.

Six months into treatment John announced trouble with his blood tests. He soon learned that he had leukemia with a prognosis of not more than 11 years of life. In a state of shock John desperately embarked on a program to find the best doctors and to participate in a holistic health program consisting of a specific diet and the use of the Symington technique. He could not come to terms with the fact that he generally felt fine while something in his body slowly killed him.

With this development I became rather discontent with the thrust of treatment still revolving around his relationship with his wife. I felt that unless we could investigate his well-submerged feelings about his mother—namely, the sense of abandonment, rage, despair, and need to hold onto her through somatization— his medical treatment might not prove terribly effective.

To make things worse, his wife chose this point, with considerable trepidation and guilt, to call a halt to the marriage. John's response was fear and a sense of abandonment on the one hand and relief that perhaps now he could explore some of his homosexual fantasies on the other. Up to that point John had been seeing me once a week, and although more frequent individual sessions would have been optimal, we decided that an added group session would best fit his financial limitations.

The disturbing prospect of a young man facing early death took its toll on me. I was vaguely aware of acting out a rescue fantasy, that somehow I would get to the bottom of his relationship with his mother and save John. I knew better, but there it was. Part of him reminded me of my son, and at the same time I could almost feel his father in the room. In weighing all of these visions and perceptions and considering that verbal associations were not getting to repressed material, I decided to take a more active role in the treatment.

I asked John to draw his mother. He found this very difficult to do in my presence, so I asked him to take home a pad and to think about his mother and to see if he could recapture some images of her. He was to bring the pictures back to me for us to discuss them.

The first week John forgot to do this; the second week he

drew but didn't bring in the pad. In the third week he appeared with the pad, and we went over the images and perceptions (Figure 10-1). The pictures were quite revealing.

The first picture was a vague image, a face in a womblike enclosure. The face seemed shrouded, with an unrelated, detached smile. Suddenly that smile reminded me of John's, and I felt I was looking at a vague, faraway identification between John and something lost.

The next picture was a back. No arms, no legs, just a back that could have belonged to anyone. John went on to try harder to recall his image of his mother.

Next came an outline of a powerful, earthy-looking woman. Her breasts and genital hair were displayed. There were no facial characteristics, arms, or legs—just the image of a powerful earth woman. This and the preceding image must have been strong ones in John's eyes, or else were used defensively in the service of warding off the tender image that would emerge with his next drawing, for he used each image once again in the ensuing two pictures. In this next drawing, a Modigliani-like figure appeared. She was sensuous, soft, touchable, with a wistful quality. Again John drew only the upper half of the body, but there was a quality of sensitivity, warmth, and tenderness hitherto missing in the drawings.

Suddenly in the next depiction the sense of true humanity evaporated, and all that was left were the sexual characteristics of pubic hair and a belly-button. I suspected that John was unable to bear the tenderness and sense of loss evoked by the Modigliani-like woman, causing a regression in form in his artwork. Where there had been an integrated, representational drawing that included a tactile sense and affective characteristics, there now was a disintegration of body level connections into a fragmentation of parts. That was to become worse in the following drawing as the page became fillled with abstract curves, unintegrated lines, and movement but no substance or organization. Further regression in form had occurred in the diffuseness and lack of definition.

It appeared that John was moving in the direction of a fusion state where the ability to distinguish between self and other was lost. His next depiction became a cellular representation of dots

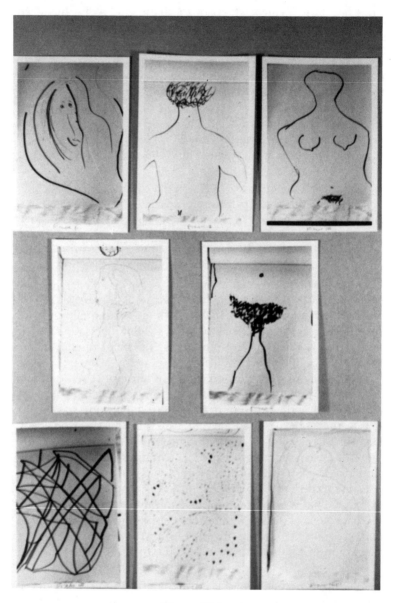

Figure 10-1.

and lines spread out throughout the entire sheet of paper, with his final picture becoming a warring jumble of criss-cross lines, reds and blacks fighting each other, no sense of synthesis, and a general disorganization of form and composition.

Looking at the series of pictures, I saw a steady regression precipitated by the unbearable sense of loss the tender mother evoked. There was a steady progression backward from whole object, to part object, to a cellular-like state where self and object were undifferentiated.

As we looked at the series of pictures, John recognized that he was cutting off his feelings, but he didn't know how to get back to them. I realized that although John was not ready at that point to explore the depth of pain and loss he was sheltering, he perhaps needed some mild confrontation. The fact that he had drawn the Modigliani-like woman meant that a full object relationship had existed at one time, although there had been a good deal of regressive activity away from that image.

Because the drawing exercises had proved to be interesting but mainly intellectual pursuits, I wondered if the affect we were struggling to reach could be found in John's world of music. A concern I had in suggesting the use of that medium was that John was so highly trained as a musician he might not be able to let go of technique to use the music as a form of raw expression. Although I had little competence in music therapy, I suspected that sound and rhythm were connected to the early mother–infant interactions. My suggestion that John try an improvisation to explore feelings related to his mother was met with curiosity and interest.

We went into the next room and John started to play. As he got into deeper, somber, sad notes, I became aware that at a certain point the music became more fanciful and technical. It was at that point that I became disengaged from the music. I commented about that, and John responded that he realized that that was exactly what he did. Too many people had told him that his music was depressing. I reemphasized that he lost my attention at the point at which he became too technical.

Back in the office we replayed a tape of the music. I asked John if he had any feelings about the music and if he would like to draw some of the images or thoughts it evoked. He proceeded to do his impression of the piece. The drawing reminded both of us of two people dancing, and it seemed like an invitation. I observed that to John. We agreed that it might be helpful to kinesthetically feel what had been visually depicted by dancing to his theme. John instructed me to mirror him, and we proceeded to dance to the music. Touched by the experience, John left the session very pleased.

In our next session John reported that he went to a party and met an older woman with whom he danced. He was reminded of our dancing together and found the dancing both erotic and sensuous. On his way home from the dance John met a man with whom he decided to engage in sex. Because my summer vacation was approaching, and both John and I were well aware of that, I was not surprised when John said that he expected his relationship to be more than a superficial affair. What he verbalized was that he felt excited and involved, scared, but wanting to explore the relationship to its fullest. He reflected again about his dance experience with me and said that I was not particularly his type but that he had found the experience "moving." I thought to myself that this newfound lover of John's was probably a transitional object to stand in for me while I was away over the summer. In fact, the relationship quickly fell apart when I returned at the end of the summer.

Our dancing together had been both an experience that became a deep meeting place, a transitional space from which other relationships could spring, but also a defensive and regressive experience in that the very primitive mirroring John had asked for was really another way of putting himself and us in a fusion state. John seemed to need a man in his life to serve as an equalizing factor against his intense pain of loss. The sexual play with his brother and later with his adolescent friend were attempts to run from his feelings of abandonment through erotic fusion. Men were the objects of his activity because they were sufficiently distant from the ambivalent lost love object, his mother. That splitting kept John functioning.

In a subsequent session we returned to the topic of music, and John wanted to try again to improvise in the attempt to recapture his experiences with his mother. As we returned to the music room, I encouraged John to go with his despair and depression and to try to ignore technical aspects as he played. I soon heard a piercing high note that weaved in and out of his music, like a theme of deep pain that touched his very depths. As he started to get near this pain, he backed away. I encouraged him to stay with the feeling and go back to it, but he cried out, "I can't, I can't." There was a profound despair in the music as he tried to continue. Finally, he broke down and repeatedly played one note, banging heavily on the piano: touching it, pushing on it until the whole room was filled with pain to the exclusion of everything else. Visibly shaken, John cried. We both had been engulfed by an experience we would never forget. As John walked back to the office, he stated in a completely depleted tone of voice, "You can talk and talk about these things, but there are some things that words can't do. This was one of them."

The next time I saw John he arrived for the session 20 minutes late. He had the runs and found it difficult to stay in the room because of his diarrhea. He wondered aloud whether he had a virus or if the condition had to do with the previous session. Did the inundating feelings of despair and loss that filled the room now break through his body armor? I mused aloud that a lot of "shit" had been released last session and that it was hard to stop once it started to flow. With discomfort John agreed.

When John again came a bit late to the next session, I felt impatient, wondering what was wrong, and commenting that our time was precious. He gave me a shy grin and said that the delay was beyond his control; the trains were late. He then returned to the drawings he had done of his mother, now replacing his former feelings of pain and loss with anger. The music released one layer of feelings to uncover another. As he looked at the images, he had the impulse to stomp on them. I cautioned him to express his anger but to preserve the drawings because he too easily identified and fused with his mother. I wanted us to have the external mirror, the pictures, to help him process his feelings. Destroying the drawings was too close to acting out, something he had had more than enough of in his life.

Respecting my desire to save the drawings, John proceeded to vent his anger and fury at his mother. "Where was she?" he complained. Then bitterly he added: "You know, you talk about my coming in five minutes late. What about you? You are going away for two whole months!" Uncomfortable about those feelings, John nonetheless did not apologize for them. We tried to explore a bit the transference issue we had just uncovered regarding anger and loss.

In the next session before I was to go away I told John that I wanted to use the material on which we had been working for a paper and needed his permission. His one provision was that he have an active part in the presentation by understanding what I was planning to do with it. He was very clear that he didn't want, yet again, to be a victim of fate. Going over the material, John made a few comments and corrections, then went on to describe technically the quality of the high note that had taken on such importance. He said, "You know, though you're not a musician, I was particularly gratified and pleased that you took the risk of wanting to work with me on the piano, even though you don't know how to play. I know from my own experience as a piano teacher that you don't have to know how to play the piano to be expressive and to play something you feel deeply."

In a way he was becoming my consultant and teacher, just as I was his teacher and therapist. There was a sense of closeness and mutuality between us. The mirror transference had moved into the real relationship. The real relationship that occurred within the therapeutic process was not aimed at changing the world outside. It did serve to help John to face the terror and loss that had remained buried in his body for so many years. As was noted, the real relationship did not preclude the emergence of transference issues as well.

Looking back at that segment of treatment, a number of factors seem evident. The pictures that John drew were only the beginning of a long search to discover his missing mother. In many respects they were intellectual exercises, and yet they did give some indication of what we would face in reconnecting with the repressed feelings relating to his mother's death. The sweetness and tenderness of the Modigliani-like image, as well as the regressive pull toward fusion, were too overwhelming to be first experienced in a visual form. With the mastery John possessed in music, that medium allowed him to better control the rate and intensity at which he would explore his profound loss, and later, anger. Music was first experienced on a defensive level with the use of technique, then moved into a deep level of expression with genuine improvisation, and then was contained and mirrored in movement and ultimately organized in visual form. I found myself wondering if music was one of the more profound ways that John made contact with his mother at some very early level. In any case, it afforded a way to get back to a bodily felt sense of loss.

The mirroring dance represented the fusing wish to be held by a man, as he had wished to gain solace and support from his father. As discussed earlier, it ended up serving both defensive and adaptive roles, but was perhaps necessary to give John the structure to go further into the process.

Art gave John the opportunity to hold the images, to contain the affects that broke through in his musical improvisation. Ultimately, it acted as a transitional bridge between affect and cognition.

In summary, we see the interplay of three different modalities at work. In all of the dimensions we see a search for a sense of self that was cut off and protected from experiencing and coming to terms with pain, loss, and anger. A more cohesive sense of self was now begun and along with it the groundwork for an inner mirror.

II

Having begun the process of pulling together the disparate pieces of his "self," John now needed to work through nuances of his internal mother and father and to find a synthesis of the polarities. I began to feel like a Dutch uncle. I challenged, confronted, cajoled, and in general was intolerant of his wish to dissociate and withdraw. At the same time I encouraged his efforts at mastery, supported him wherever he showed strength, and mirrored or reflected the feelings that joined both of us in a mutual process. I remember wondering whether I was gratifying his need for a strong masculine ideal. John, for his part, responded well to this approach, and material unfolded with a minimum of resistance (Figures 10-2).

In order to give the reader a sense of the flow of the nonverbal material, the drawings and his accompanying comments

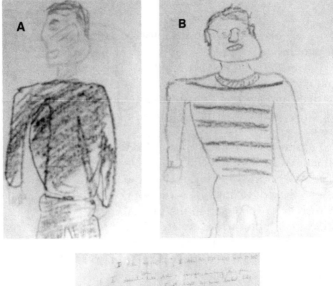

Figure 10-2.   AR as he is; AR as I'd like him to be. (A): Doesn't look
   like AR—younger, smiling, thin face, midsection, and legs. First
   draft, top torso looked like a tooth (Dad). (B): Also doesn't look
   like AR, but rather like SB (fantasy image: heavier, broader),
   wearing SB's colors, blues rather than drab olives and browns AR
   usually wears. (C): The brooding, slinking, schlumpy, dark side
   of AR is missing.

will be presented in serial form. Much of the nonverbal work was done at home and was brought into the next session for discussion. For the most part, drawings were accompanied by music that the patient composed relating to a theme that emerged in sessions.

The new phase in therapy was begun with a drawing of Harry (Figure 10-3A), his eighteen-year-old lover, who expands into the page's space. John talked about the purple locked into Harry's body as his personal color of eroticism. There is a power and ferocity in this figure that both frightened and intrigued John. Despite all of his efforts, he couldn't capture the sweetness of the relationship. The depiction of Harry's mouth betrayed the underlying hostility of the artist. The hostility, along with fear, erupted into John's consciousness as he contemplated his creation. He also struggled with the inappropriateness of his choice. Harry was a runaway truant who did not want to be tied down; he was unpredictable and irresponsible. The patient made every effort to possess his lover, but the real image of Harry eluded him. I challenged John. Was the image of Harry a projection of his own disowned wish for power? Could he tolerate the brutality that slipped in along with the sweetness? John moved away from the relationship and was left with both a sense of perplexity and a greater awareness of his own needs for a stable relationship.

Remember the purple, for it reappears over and over in the drawings, reflecting the eroticism he used to run from pain. Sexuality offered him a place in which he could fuse and feel a sense of oneness, perhaps even lose himself.

Next John drew a picture of his wife (Figure 10-3B). Although she looked wooden and stiff, she had a solidity and warmth to her that was reminiscent of his much earlier primitive earth mother. He was struck by the distortions between his drawing and his wife, who was less robust and wore her hair differently. Most apparent, though, was the difference in feeling tone. His conscious feelings for his wife contained none of the warmth his drawing depicted. It became clearer why John struggled so hard for a male ideal to compensate for his own weak, passive father: he needed to find masculine strength to coun-

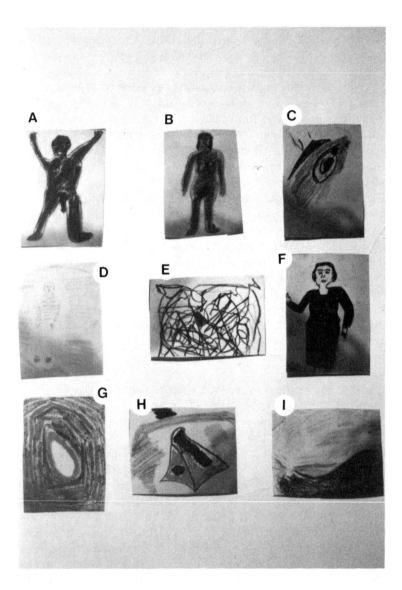

Figure 10-3A. 1. Powerful, lively, sexual. 2. When put teeth into mouth, what had seemed like a smile turned into anger, or ferocious mouth. 3. Didn't capture his grace and lightness, flow; mostly represented his strength and held-in anger. This sometimes frightens me. (This was drawn shortly after a phone conversation where we argued more than we have before). 4. Harry has a tremendous amount of sweetness; this isn't in picture. 5. There is a kind of dark purple in his coloring that I wanted to convey. 6. As soon as I started, I realized that he would be naked. I often visualize him nude (he often is at home). (a) His dick had been one of the lightest parts; so was his face (to avoid obliterating details). I don't see him that way, so darkened both. The result is that his dick is now the darkest area. 7. The picture frightens yet invigorates me. I'm surprised that my tenderness I feel toward him doesn't seem to show. *(1—All captions are statements written by the patient next to his drawings.)*

Figure 10-3B. 1. There's a warmth from (and toward?) Kate, especially in her face. Ironically, her face, with its "frown" often seems harsh and cold. Is this a fantasy?. 2. Her body seems wooden, lifeless. (a) She's drawn much heavier and bulkier than she is (more masculine?) 3. As with Harry, the hands and feet are very clublike. 4. She has more "curves" than earlier drawings of my mother. 5. Her coloring is a mustard, which is close to life. 6. Her hair is drawn differently than she ever wore it. I always preferred her Afro. (She thinks because it's more masculine.) I tried to draw her with braids, the way she wore hair when we first met. There were positive aspects of our relationship at the beginning that disappeared, became less supportive, affectionate.

Figure 10-3C. MY CANCER, 1. Looks like a white blood cell. (a) I had spoken to Onifer's father today and then read some basic information on cancer and realized that I had erroneously thought of my diagnosis as cancer of the blood-forming cells in the bone marrow. Actually, it's the lymph and spleen production of W.B.'s that are giving me trouble. (My visualization and hypno-suggestion will change accordingly.) 2. This is only one cell—overcomeable, yet it's very large with intense red and black core. 3. Picture occupies top and center of page, very prominent. 4. Looks like something is invading cell, a kind of moving bullet. It hasn't begun to penetrate the central core of the cell but is just about to. 5. Looks a little like a tooth. I associate that with Dad.

Figure 10-3D.   DAD IN GRAYS & WHITE, I. MUSIC, 1. Started soft, wistful. Image of him as not forceful, definitive, not dynamic. 2. Began to feel too limited by those boundaries; "wanted more color," therefore introduced some dissonance and stronger playing—more feeling—dynamics, sense of rhythm. Builds, then 3. Started to play repeated note with chord on presentation tape of my mother but here note repeats faster and moves upward. Doesn't sound stuck. Goes on to something else. 4. Ends with a short, fragmented, lonely theme. MOTHER IN RED AND BLACK, I. MUSIC, 1. Rhythmic, driving. Tension of underlying ostinato and melody over. Anxious. 2. Becomes denser, quicker. 3. Brief, soft dance. 4. Started to go into slow, pretty sad melody—didn't want to do that "again." Went elsewhere. 5. Return to ostinato-like beginning. 6. Frenzied clusters of notes till ending chord cuts off sustained sounds.

#1: Figure 10-3E.   DRAWING, 1. When started to listen to tape while drawing—took a color in each hand and "scribbled" simultaneously. Soon realized that this was supposed to be representational but decided to keep going. Darkened same areas after. At end of music (when frantic), felt anxious and had to darken a triangle area in the center. This area enables me to focus on it instead of scrambling all over picture, which seems like a maze. Also the reds and blacks are so intertwined it feels as if I'm merged with my mother. I don't know if I'm the red or the black. Toward the center, I see an image that reminds me of a woman, dancing or gliding (in red). If I'm one of the colors—am I then the black? Is that death?

#2: Figure 10-3F.   1. Feels more like a grandmother. 2. Even though in red and black—doesn't have strong feeling. Whole process took 1½ hours. I want to stop now.

Figure 10-3G.   PAIN (No. 1), 1. Overwhelming, covers my whole vision (fills the sheet). 2. Layers, deeper, deeper—center is gray and white, Dad's color theme, around that the red of mother (and life energy), which is therefore trapped by the pain. 3. Music tried to break out of pain, sadness (they're merged) at times. In listening to it while drawing, I coaxed it on saying: "break out, break out." (a) Always went back to the pain. 4. Brilliance to the colors. 5. After finished playing, felt like I was just scratching the surface. (Though I felt sad when I began, I didn't cry throughout). (a) Immediately played another piece. When drawing, I finished this one while listening to first piece.

Figure 10-3H.   PAIN (No. 2), 1. After doing drawing No. 1 (while listening to tape), I felt that at least pain allows me to feel something; makes me feel alive even though it hurts. It's my main connection to feelings; it's what I feel if I'm feeling anything. That made me feel better. (a) Even though music in No. 2 is quite painful, my drawing isn't. 2. I looked at purple crayon as I started and it felt erotic—the intensity of the color and its phallic shape. I started with that. Blue on either side came next, then green. After that I felt a need to have more connection, using orange to connect the blues. (Then filled in pink, yellow and purple circle). (a) There's also more space. 3. The music has a connectedness, too. Continuous tempo, one key (G minor); most of other music moves from key to key.

Figure 10-3I.   PAIN (No. 3) Turn Out the Stars—Composition by Bill Evans w/improvisation 1. The sea. No people. Feel very sad, lonely. Started to cry a little. 2. Became intense when I visualized Yvonne. Cried and said: "I love you, Kate."

terbalance the internal primitive, powerful earth woman he projected on all women.

Meanwhile, John received more medical information that clarified the nature of his condition. What he thought had been a cancer of the blood-forming cells in the bone marrow was actually a cancer of white blood cell production in lymph glands and spleen. With that information he changed the images in his visualization exercises and drew a cancer cell (Figure 10-3C). This single cell was gray with a red and black inner core. He noted that a bullet-like object was invading the cell. His association to the drawing was of a tooth, which in turn made him think of his father. The themes of gray versus red and black as being representative of father and mother, respectively, were hinted at but not developed.

John tried a picture of his father, and a withdrawn, wistful picture emerged in gray and white (Figure 10-3D). Moving to the piano, John was aware of the lack of forcefulness, definition, and dynamism in his rendering and felt limited by those boundaries. Running from those feelings, John added dissonance to his music, hoping to introduce more "color" but ended with a short lonely theme. Where he could attempt to modify his image of his father in music, he could not yet transfer that color to paper.

Now mother took center stage in an intense discordant tension of red and blacks, with a triangle in the middle of a woman dancing (Figure 10-3E). Red was his mother, with all the vitality and life he associated with her, but always paired with the red was the black of death and despair. The reds and blacks pounded away at one another in a frenzy of pain and emotion. As much as John would lament and fight against what he felt was an unbearable amount of pain, he also realized that with the pain he was most alive and related.

A very clear image of grandma now erupted into his consciousness, organizing both colors (Figure 10-3F). Fusion allowed for separateness; disorganization and disintegration gave way to a new level of consciousness. John wasn't sure what to say about her, but there's no denying the forthright and forceful image on the page.

This seemed to allow more associations with his mother to emerge, and he shared experiences about her that were both touching and moving. He brought in photographs of family life and remembered loving feelings he had held for his mother. He also remembered her as being a very dominant and alive force in the family. The powerful earth mother who needed center stage found her way more and more often into the sessions.

Pain now became the focus, with three renderings and associated music. In Pain No. 1 (Figure 10-3G) there was a layering of color with gray and white at its center, surrounded by red and finally purple. John readily identified the gray as his father and red as mother and noted that the life energies were trapped by pain. Moving to the piano, John tried to break out of the pain, but the theme kept returning. Again, purple was the eroticism he would use defensively against the internal struggle.

John tried to modify the pain in the picture and music of Pain No. 2 (Figure 10-3H). He killed the grays, blacks, and intense reds, and in their places used a lot of purple and introduced pink. Being well aware of the sexuality, John noted that the phallic purple crayon made him "feel erotic." Even with the color changes, the picture remained contained and segmented as John fled into eroticism to avoid the pain.

Pain No. 3 (Figure 10-3I) became a blue and green sea with no people. John felt lonely and sad here and began to cry. As the pain intensified, he visualized his wife and said, "I love you." This, in turn, reminded him of his picture of his mother with the dancer imbedded in the triangle.

John now drew a picture called "Wife Dancing" (Figures 10-4A, B) but quickly realized it was really his mother he wanted to see dance, be vibrant and alive. He noted that the left breast had been blurred, the breast his mother had had removed. What emerged was a purple dancer with a black tornado on the right side, a phallic ice-pick menacing on the left, and anger—a lot of anger as he pounded in the dots.

Looking at that picture, I noted the best form of any drawn so far, with the use of purple, his eroticism, on a female figure for the first time. He also used black to reflect destruction rather than death. With each regression and expression of rage came more differentiation.

The to and fro between female and male, maternal and paternal images continued as John, in his attempt to depict a more differentiated view of his childhood world, drew a pallid "Good Humor man" in gray (Figure 10-4C). He recognized the metaphor as the father who had never offered John any frame or mirror in which to explore his own vitality or strength. Lacking it in himself, music had been his phallic power, the place where vitality and life could find expression. Here he found a connection that affirmed the self.

With this recognition, John first added a red streak coming

Figure 10-4A.   KATE'S DANCE, 1. Had dance on my mind having just spoken to Juan about future possible collaboration (he's a dancer, choreographer). 2. Going to Y's for dinner later this evening. 3. Music rhythmic, jazzy, bluesy. 4. Dancer doesn't look like Kate. Is someone else doing "her dance?" (Jean) (a) Had attempted to "draw Kate's hair, eyebrows, etc.," but looks like someone else. 5. Left breast had to be redone, didn't come out right first time—too small and crooked. Mommy's left breast was removed. This mommy? (Didn't call her mom or mother. Something childlike—mommy). 6. Black section at right came first—tornado, arc in Japanese gardens. 7. Music driving now. Had wish to see her dance. Felt like she was my mother and I wanted to see her move—be alive, vibrant. 8. Orange at left—phallic, flowing, yet menacing, like an ice pick. 9. Music makes me feel alive, especially when rhythmic. Even the slow parts seem to be searching. A lot of blues here; blues is feeling music. This music makes me feel strong, sexual. (a) Physical need at end of drawing to grab fistful of crayons and "pound in" the dots. Felt a little angry at that point. For a split second, envision covering drawing completely, obliterating dancer.

Figure 10-4B.   FOR KATE (COMPOSITION), Written for her about 8 years ago 1. Similar pose as previous "Kate," which looked like my mother. 2. She feels blurry, not clear, can't define her. 3. Music has drive and tension—polyrhythms, 4/3, 5/3 yet lyrical. 4. She's "locked in" in drawing. No feet—like she's sinking. 5. Used some of her colors (autumn, earth).

Figure 10-4C.   1. More free associated last session—didn't try to draw well. Childlike perception. 2. My face looks like a skull (death-like). Started to draw one ear, it looked funny; didn't draw other. (a) Didn't want to "hear" music "For Kate." She brought up divorce on Saturday night. If I don't want to get back together, she wants a divorce. I said I didn't want to get back. 3. Just added a red streak from door of my house to me as a kid. I was looking at red crayon. Had image from "The Fourth Man," a visually brilliant movie. Theme of women as possessing evil powers. (a) Red is bloodlike but also vibrant. The rest is grays, (Dad), black, purple child. Needs life. 4. Good Humor man (Irving) reminded me of Dad. (Also gray). He seemed to genuinely like kids. Is warm in drawing. (a) Association to June's Dad (dying?) with CLL. I called Baltimore this week and spoke with him. I was thrown off when he said, "I love you." I said I love him too, yet it didn't totally feel real. I hardly know him. 5. My house doesn't look too inviting. (I visited old neighborhood with Jean weekend). 6. No one on the street or in houses. A kind of ghost buildings. 7. These notes are intentionally more freely associated.

Figure 10-4D.   SEPARATING FROM KATE, 1. I'm always using the piano to "feel" with, to fuck with. (a) Shape drawn between us quickly became a piano. It's thrusting up toward Kate like a dick. 2. I was hairless at first. Gave me sad feeling of having lost my hair (chemo). I first put green on my head, then black, (what it used to be), then gray, then white. (a) Felt positive that I took action—coloring in hair. (b) Ambivalence about hair color. (Hair stylists always say, I wish I had your color hair, but I want it

dark.) 3. Doesn't look like me or Kate. (a) Me, big-headed, thick-necked (like my brother). (b) We're both smiling; reaching out to each other (incident during week). 4. Felt sad playing. Started free improvisation—moved into "Midnight," K & my "song," first song I ever played for her. (a) I once played this for Kate while crying in response to a "heavy" (separation?) discussion. I couldn't express feelings verbally. She said she was tired of my not being verbal. "How do you respond to this?" (she said to my playing this). 5. My playing here becomes increasingly fragmented and harsher, often angry.

out of the house to himself and the Good Humor man, then talked about a movie of women possessing evil powers. There was an attempt here to bring together the red of blood and rage with vibrancy and to introduce it into the gray world of his father; in other words, to bring vibrancy into his own life in a way that didn't become anxiety provoking. What seemed to happen each time he approached that kind of synthesis was that in connecting with the lusty world of his mother he also connected with cancer and death and was terrified at being trapped there.

John continued to feel guilty at witholding from his wife and separating from her but felt no desire to return to the relationship. Drawing "Separating from Wife," (Figure 10-4D), John put a piano between the two of them and noted again that music and the piano had served as his phallus. He did add some red to himself for the first time, perhaps starting to realize that vibrancy and power may come not only from piano playing but also from saying good-bye, putting to rest, metaphorically, the internal representations he had carried of women and his mother. Interestingly, in coloring the hair on himself (which was actually gray) he used first green then black. Although slowly coming to terms with the mother inside, I suspected that John was still trying to avoid any identification with his father.

As he started talking about separation, John thought of a childhood friend playing with a stickball. He drew that image (Figure 10-5A) and commented, "I want to suck his dick." Passive-regressive issues were still very much present in this need of John's to search for a childhood friend and grab his power as soon as John started to separate.

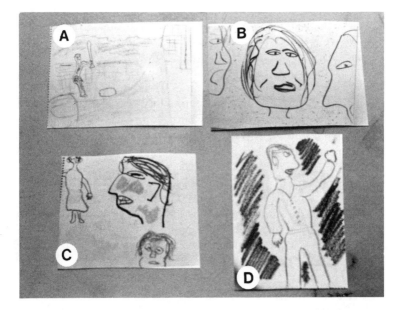

Figure 10-5A. VIEW ACROSS STREET WHERE I GREW UP
1. Jim at bat, playing stickball. He's naked. I often imagined him
nude while playing stickball. Drawing this has been a turn on for
me. I want to suck his dick and then fuck him (a) The bat is more
like a baseball bat which we never used (more phallic?). We used
broomsticks. 2. This point-of-view shot. I'm the yellow and orange. Yellow mass started picture then drew Jim. 3. Music is
building (with suspended chords). (a) I'm feeling I want Jim to
fuck me. Jim's image merges with my brother's. Music sexually
climatic. Image returns to Jim, romantic, holding him after sex.
This is fantasy, never really happened like that, though we had
sexual play a number of times. I wanted much more.

**Figure 10-5B,C,D.   Figure in red felt like Kate. I feel some guilt about
having a relationship with a woman. (If I could work out some
of my anger at M, shouldn't it be with Kate?)**

The final trio of drawings were struggles with red and black. First there was another drawing of his wife in red (Figure 10-5B), which keyed into the intense guilt he felt in separating. The last two were self-portraits in red and black showing himself first in a side view of the face (Figure 10-5C), then in a full-view portrait with feet cut off (Figure 10-5D). He was facing the fact that he was not only a good, sweet little boy, but also a very angry one. Perhaps his self-imposed immobility reflected his need to protect others from his hostility and sadism.

Throughout all of these explorations, John's musical ability and horizons expanded, as he started to create words for his songs. He was invited to collaborate in putting together an operetta from a number of personal pieces associated with his feelings related to the loss of his mother through cancer. The complete set of those song/poems is in the Appendix, but I want to include here one of particular poignancy. Entitled "Forgiveness and Death," it is a wrenching piece that puts John in the place of his dying mother.

Can you forgive me for needing to be alone,
Just when you want me to hold you.
Can you forgive me for not hearing you when you ask
If birds live in the sky.
Can you forgive me
For being too tired to tuck you in at night
Please forgive me. Please forgive me.

Can you forgive me
For being so bitter I poison your games.
Can you forgive me
For being so angry I forgot how to laugh.
Can you forgive me
For crying each time I look in your eyes.
Please forgive me. Please forgive me.

We leave this patient in process as he faces his own vibrancy as well as the darker part of his rage, and separates from some of the more destructive identifications with his father. His sense of power and feelings of mastery have expanded into areas of real accomplishment. The sexual part of him still has a long way to go, however, to be integrated with the true life form of this man. There is still the work of uncovering the projective identification of a phallic ideal. His wife still implores in one of his pictures, "Where are you? Define yourself [in words]."

John's sadism and rage still frighten him, and he requires much mirroring of his authentic masculine aspirations. Rhythm, music, and movement seem to be embodied in the image of his mother and captured in the intensity of his music. Now the vibrancy must find avenues into his relationships with others.

Medically, he is more than holding his own and has even surprised his doctors in terms of the progress of his condition. Neither the patient nor I knows what his future will hold, but I support and affirm his wish to take power and control of his life and to live it fully now matter how long he has to live.

Chapter 11

A FINAL WORD

All of us who are mental health professionals are also art therapists in the sense that each and every one of us struggles to rise above the boundaries of words, to hone skills associated with the aesthetics of communication. What the creative arts therapist has brought to the mental health field in particular is the notion that psychodynamics and principles of aesthetics are intricately interwoven and that by tapping the artist within ourselves and our patients we have an invaluable treatment tool.

However, the logistics of receiving training in this integrated verbal/nonverbal approach is problematic. Advanced training programs are often manned by psychiatrists or psychologists who have little identification or empathy with issues that speak to the very heart and soul of the artist in the therapist. Indeed, the orientation of these programs is often statistically oriented and cannot easily be reshaped to investigate the subtleties of the processes of creative and therapeutic communications. At the same time, we do have much to learn from these disciplines.

Essentially, the problem comes down to a very basic question: how can we translate the language of psychology into a language of art? In this text I have offered examples of recasting object relations theory into visual contexts. However, as therapists become more adept at looking at psychodynamics as they manifest themselves in aesthetic forms, classical verbal orientations of all kinds will be enriched and reshaped. As that happens, it will become more and more imperative that psychology courses for therapists interested in this integrated approach be taught by teachers who themselves have nonverbal grounding.

Currently, such training is basically the province of graduate creative-arts therapy programs, which creates further problems. Very real political and legal dilemmas face the therapists who come out of those programs as art, dance, and music therapists. Often creative-arts therapists enter advanced training programs to prepare themselves for private practice. With the notable exception of California, most states do not legally recognize a master's degree in creative-arts therapy, rendering creative-arts therapists ineligible for third-party reimbursement. What good does it do to preserve our language if we cannot practice with the training offered us? Why go into one of the rare advanced training programs manned by creative-arts therapists if it does not provide legal recognition? With such complex political, sociological, and economic ramifications, it is hardly a wonder that so many creative-arts therapists complete training programs that are strictly verbal in nature and leave their artists' roots behind in the process. The pity is that those roots meet such resistance when they are transplanted in the hopes of producing rich new hybrids.

As teachers and established therapists, we cannot afford to hide from the social and political realities facing our students and future colleagues when they leave master's-level programs. If we are to hold onto the option of training future professionals who elicit the artists in themselves and in their patients in private practice, then we have a responsibility to help them receive the political and legal recognition necessary to function. That recognition can be obtained only when we work together as nonverbal professionals to translate our dreams into the reality of concrete political action.

Those of us who work with psychodynamics in aesthetic forms have a tool that demands nourishment and protection. We need to develop our own language and theoretical framework, but we must also be conversant in the language of other professionals. We must seek legal protection for our unique skills while continuing to remain receptive to the contributions of our colleagues. Ultimately, if we are to grow as professionals, we must develop concepts and formulations to match the complexities and depths of our therapeutic experiences. This text has been an attempt to make a small contribution in that area.

APPENDIX

BEFORE

My child, you are my love
Dear one, you are my life
Running across the park
hearing us laugh together
Feeling your smile, watching you grow
Helps me forget pain many years ago
Child you are my love. Dear one, you are my life
Come let us dance while birds fly above
Child you are my love
Dear one you are my life

SOMETHING'S WRONG

Something's wrong I can feel it down deep
Don't need a doctor to tell me
But just what is it? Even they can't say.

This cough won't stop
Keeps me up all night
Probably should stop smoking, I know
But can't, too tense now

Maybe it'll go away
These things often do
I'm jumping to conclusions again
It's probably nothing, nothing at all
And yet I can't help feeling
Something's wrong, I'm all out of phase
Something's wrong, I can feel it down deep
Deep down
Something's wrong.

CANCER

I can't take another test
Please don't siphon any more blood
Tubes reach inside my lungs
X-rays peer inside my being
The very marrow of my bones can't hide
They've more than raped me.
As I wait for more test results
I feel unreal
Like a game of cards and they always deal
Will this time be the same?
Inconclusive answers
Don't worry—told with a purple smile

This anxiety is driving me completely mad
Not knowing is the worst thing of all
I'd almost rather have death looking into my eyes
Than face an uncertain life ahead.

I can't stand this pounding, this pounding in my chest
Gotta keep moving
Yet wind up in the same place, no space
Exploding blood, the taste of volcanic ash
Metal grinds my groin
splitting, reeling, bursting.

Here comes the doctor
Do I really want to know?
I've got what?

Cancer. . .cancer. . .cancer. . .cancer. . .cancer
What are you talking about?
No!. . .cancer. . .cancer
It's not fair, that couldn't be.
No. No.
Why me? What did I do?
Damn it. . .damn it. . .damn it. . .damn it

CONFLICTING NEEDS

I hear you calling me. But
I need all of my energy to take care of my self
                    "

Why do I have to choose between your needs and mine
Can't you understand? Won't you try? 'cause
I need all of my energy to take care of myself
                    "

I've always been strong, I've had to. They needed
                me that way
Since I was a child, as the oldest of four
I had to take care of the rest
Then when popa died:
I need all of my energy to take care of myself.
I never had to depend on anyone; no one was there anyway
Mama was so withdrawn.
Part of me, always wanted to be taken care of.
But not because of this.
I need all of my energy to take care of myself.

What's left but a strong facade
crumbling, crumbling inside
And you're too young to understand
And your father's too scared to try.
I know what a mother should do
But I can't continue doing it for much longer
For once I've got to look out for me
I feel so guilty

I need all of my energy to take care of myself
I need, you I need, yes I need someone there for me.

FORGIVENESS AND DEATH

Can you forgive me for needing to be alone,
just when you want me to hold you.
Can you forgive me for not hearing you when you ask
If birds live in the sky
Can you forgive me
For being too tired to tuck you in at night
Please forgive me. Please forgive me.

Can you forgive me
For being so bitter I poison your games
Can you forgive me
For being so angry I forgot how to laugh
Can you forgive me
For crying each time I look in your eyes.
Please forgive me. Please forgive me.

LOVE SONG

Oh how I love you
words can't describe just how I
Feel as your hand reaches out towards mine
They join together softly
Though you're not sure
Yes how I love you

Once I helped you catch a brilliant butterfly
And when it flew away
You cried and cried until you realized
How your life had changed
Just by seeing its beauty.

Now remember I love you
I'm so glad that you forgive me
And now this love can last
Past your life and mine.

Now remember I love you
I'm so glad that you forgive me
And now this love can last
Past your life and mine.

IF I WERE TO DIE TOMORROW

If I were to die tomorrow
I'd know I had planted a seed;
And I'd rest so content and watch my seed grow,
And remember the good times we had.

If I were to die tomorrow
I'd know I had planted a seed;
And I'd rest so content in sweet, sweet sleep,
And remember the good times we've had.
If I were to die tomorrow.

REFERENCES

Bion, W. R. (1977). Attacks on linking. In *Second thoughts*. London: Heinemann, pp. 110–119.

Deri, S. (1984). *Symbolization and creativity*. New York: International Universities Press.

Honig, S., & Haynes, K. (1982). Structured art therapy with the chronic patient in long-term residential treatment. *The Arts in Psychotherapy*, 9, 269–289.

Horner, A. (1979). *Object relations and the developing ego in therapy*. New York: Jason Aronson.

Horney, K. (1945). *Our inner conflicts*. New York: W. W. Norton.

Kernberg, O. (1976). *Borderline conditions and pathological narcissism*. New York: Science House.

LaMonica, M., & Robbins, A. (1980). Creative exploration of countertransference experiences. In Robbins, A. 1980. *Expressive therapies*, pp. 58–72. New York: Human Sciences Press.

Mahler, M. S., Pine, F., & Bergman, A. (1975). *The psychological birth of the human infant*. New York: Basic Books.

Masterson, J. (1976). *Psychotherapy of the borderline adult*. New York: Brunner/Mazel.

McDougall, J. (1980). *Pleae for measure of normality*. New York: International Universities Press.

Piaget, J. (1936). *The origins of intelligence in children*. New York: International Universities Press, 1952.

Robbins, A. (1984). A creative arts approach to art therapy. *The Arts in Psychotherapy, 2*(1), pp. 7–14.

Robbins, A. (1984). The struggle for self-cohesion. *Journal of the American Art Therapy Association, 1*(3), pp. 107–108.

Robbins, A. (1982) Integrating the personal and theoretical splits in the struggle towards an identity as art therapist. *The Arts in Psychotherapy, 9*:pp. 1–9.

Robbins, A. (1980). *Expressive therapy: A creative arts approach to depth oriented treatment*. New York: Human Sciences Press.

Robbins, A., & Sibley, L. (1976). *Creative art therapy*. New York: Brunner/Mazel.

Rubin, J. (Ed.). (in press). *Approaches to art therapy and technique*. New York: Brunner/Mazel.

Sarte, J.-P. (1964). *Nausea* (L. Alexander, Trans.). New York: New Directions. (Original work published 1938).

Segal, H. (1980). *Melanie Klein*. New York: Viking Press.

Simonton, C. (1978). *Getting well again*. New York: St. Martin Press.

Winnicott, D. W. (1971). *Playing and reality*. New York: Basic Books.

INDEX

Abstraction, 105, 113–114, 178
Acting out
  in adolescents, 58
  in children, 57
  in therapists, 127, 190
Adolescence, 58–59
Aesthetics, 14, 15, 16, 21, 43,
  61
  building blocks of, 105–115
  definition of, 22
  developmental nature of, 23
  and ego functioning, 106
  of healing, 89–103, 173
  synthesis with psychodynamics,
    89, 104, 138–139, 212–213
  of therapeutic communication,
    105, 174
      case study, 28–34
Affect mood disorder, 25, 45

Aggression, 68, 70
  in adolescence, 58
Anger, 58, 68, 85, 87, 151, 163,
  166, 178
  case study, 187–211
Anxiety, 25, 43, 149
  in adolescents, 58
Autism, 45, 107, 114

Balance, 105
Bion, W. R., 176–177
Borderline personality, 25, 35,
  45, 49–51, 114
Burnout, 117–118, 137

Cancer, 187, 189, 201, 203–204,
  216–217

Cancer (*cont.*)
    treatment of terminal patients
        with, 60
Case studies
    aesthetics of pain, 187–211
    aesthetics and psychodynamics,
        90–103
    aesthetics of therapeutic
        communication, 28–34
    holding environment, 62–88
    protective adaptations, 179–
        186
    transference/
        countertransference, 152–172
Children
    and transference issues, 57
    treatment of, 56–57, 141
Clay, 107, 178, 180–184, 185
Color, 105, 107–109, 139
Communication, 23, 150, 174,
        179
    body, 177–178
    impoverishment of, 176
    as self-disclosure, 44
    styles of, 27, 43–44, 106
    through colors, 108
    verbal versus nonverbal,
        40–41, 172
Countertransference, 133–134,
        137, 138, 179
    definition of, 148
    and transference, 147–174
Creative Art Therapy (Robbins &
        Sibley), 105

Death, 59, 71, 72, 210, 218, 219
Defensive structures, 25, 39, 47,
        106, 149
    in adolescence, 59
    and deprivation, 94
    in schizoid character, 65, 93

therapists', 117, 141, 150
    treatment of, 55
Denial, 25, 50, 149
    in depression, 65
    in schizoid character, 64
    in substance abuse, 56
    in terminal patients, 59
Depression, 13, 49, 64, 92, 151,
        155
    and mirroring, 53–54
    in terminal patients, 60
Diagnosis
    developmental, 39, 44
    in substance abuse, 55
Diffusion, 47
Drawing materials, 109

Ego, 24–25
    and aesthetic form, 106
    in borderline personality,
        50–51
    defenses, 25, 106
    in depression, 54
    levels, 41, 107
    in narcissistic personality, 51
    needs, in schizophrenics, 47
    in psychosis, 55
    skills, 138
    in substance abuse, 55
    therapist's, 49
Eliot, T. S., 100
Eroticism, 152, 199, 205

Families, of terminal patients, 60
Fantasy play, 114
Form, 105, 106
Fragmentation, 25, 139, 149
Freud, Sigmund, 147, 148
Fusion, 22, 23, 40, 45, 47, 49,
        91, 94–101, 111

Grief, 60, 64
Guilt, 14, 25, 70

Haynes, K., 47
Homosexuality, 184, 189, 190,194
Honig, S., 47
Horner, A., 44–45, 62, 93, 97,
    98, 99
Horney, Karen, 70
Hostility, 55

Id forces, 24
Idealized self, 68, 70
Illness, physical, 98–99
Introjection, 25, 50, 67, 70, 149

Jung, C. G., 108

Kernberg, O., 49
Klein, Melanie, 93

Mahler, Margaret, 26
Masterson, J., 49
McDougall, Joyce, 178
Metalwork, 111
Metaphor, 41
Mirroring transference, 51–56,
    165, 196
  principles of, 52–53
Mother-child relationship, 25,
    26, 94, 148–149, 177, 193
  and bipolar bridge, 27
Motor skills, 112–113
Mourning, 54
Movement, 105, 112–113
Music, 193–197, 205, 206–207,
    208, 211

Narcissistic personality, 25, 45, 51
  in institutions, 123, 125, 128

Object relations, 24–26, 36, 114,
    212–213
  in depression, 54
Obsessive-compulsive personality,
    54–55
Overidealization, 25, 50, 150

Pain, 149, 150, 197, 203, 204–
    205
  and therapy, 36, 199
Paranoid character, 73, 83, 85,
    87, 93
Passive-aggressive character, 55
Physical contact, 44
Piaget, Jean, 114, 178–179
Plastic materials, 107
Play, 28, 177, 179; see also
    Fantasy play
Projection, 25, 50, 149

Rage; see Anger
Rapp, Elaine, 112
Rejection, 76, 80, 81–82, 87

Sandbox play, 111
Schizoid character, 45, 49, 64–
    65, 70–71, 85, 92, 93, 151
Schizophrenia, 47, 55, 68
Secondary-process thinking, 25,
    36
Self-cohesion, 49, 51
Self-destructiveness, 14
Self-disclosure, 43–44
Self-esteem
  and depression, 49, 51

Self-esteem (*cont.*)
  and mother-child relationship,
    177
Self-object relations, 16, 38, 113
Separation, 22, 50, 94, 113, 118,
    177
Separation-individuation, 40, 94,
    107, 110, 111, 126, 131
Sexuality, 70, 82, 189, 194, 199
  in adolescence, 58
Simonton, C., 60
Somatization, 99
Space, 105, 111–112
Splitting, 25
  of psyche and soma, 177–178
Stone, working with, 110
Substance abuse, 55–56
Superego, 24, 67
  defenses, 25
Symbiosis, 26, 45–47
  in autism, 45, 46
  in schizophrenia, 46–47
Symbols, 21
  and abstraction, 113–114, 178
  and aesthetic reorganization,
    39
  and borderline personality,
    114
  communication in, 27, 39, 41,
    106

developmental nature of, 22,
    23, 89
final synthesis of, 59
and psyche-soma split, 177
in therapy, 50, 150

Texture, 105, 106–107
Transference
  and countertransference, 147–
    174, 176
  mirroring, 51–56, 165, 196
Treatment team, 129–132

Verbalization, 40–41, 138
  in adolescents, 58
  in children, 57
  in schizoid character, 65
Volume, 105, 110–111

Watercolor, 109, 112
Winnicott, D. W., 27–28, 148,
    176, 177, 178, 179
Withdrawal, 25, 47, 50, 86, 98
  in adolescents, 58
  in substance abuse, 55, 56
Woodcarving, 111